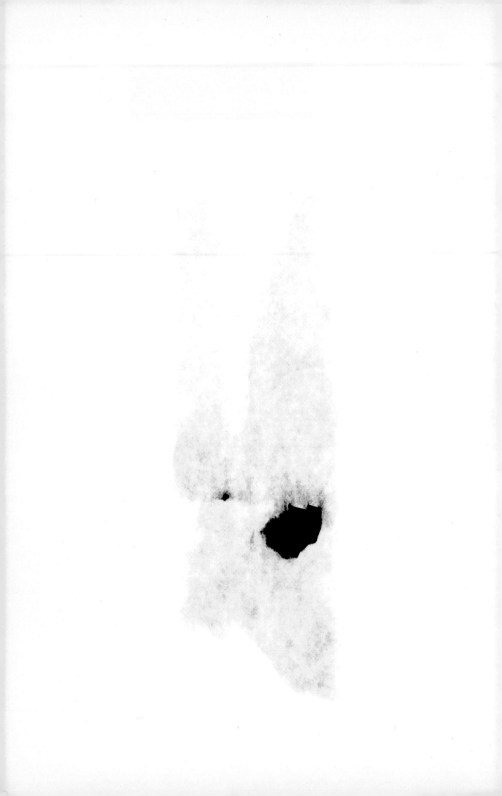

Also by Gerald B. Nelson

Changes of Heart
Ten Versions of America

Seattle

Seattle

The Life and Times
of an American City

by Gerald B. Nelson

Alfred A. Knopf
New York | 1977

THIS IS A BORZOI BOOK
PUBLISHED BY ALFRED A. KNOPF, INC.

The majority of the interviews contained in this book were conducted during
1972. They reflect the opinions and occupations of the interviewees at that
time.

Grateful acknowledgment is made to *Ramparts* magazine for permission to
reprint excerpts from pages 56, 67–8 of *Ramparts* magazine, May, 1972, Vol. 10,
No. 11. Copyright © 1972 by Noah's Ark, Inc.

Manufactured in the United States of America
First Edition

Library of Congress Cataloging in Publication Data
Nelson, Gerald B.
Seattle: the life and times of an American city.
1. Seattle—History. I. Title.
F899.S457N44   1977   979.7'77   76–47937

For my aunt, Queena Davison Miller,
and my father, L. John Nelson

Contents

Acknowledgments

I would like to thank the following who offered their time and honest opinions:

Terry Pettus, Eugene Dennett, John Conroy, Ken Baxter, Harry Briggs, Paul Wysocki, Bill Brammer, Burt Laird, Chuck Eberhardt, Wayne Nelson, Tom Beyers, Rick Locke, Wanda Adams, Peter Schnurman, Mike McManus, Neal and Ruth Buchan, Bill Roche, Jack Driscoll, Joe Quaranta, Gene Beckwith, Elizabeth Morris, George Tokuda, Marvin Burke, Bill Woo, Bill Jeske, Maynard Johnston, Henry Broderick, Peter Bush, Horace MacCurdy, William Allen, Ken MacDonald, Brewster Denny, John Gillingham, Fitzgerald Beaver, and Warren Holtz.

I am especially grateful to Alix Nelson, who conducted the interviews that appear in this book.

Seattle

Seattle, Washington

At a distance of twenty miles from our camp we halted at a village of Wahkiacums, consisting of seven ill-looking houses, built in the same form with those above, and situated at the foot of the high hills on the right, behind two small marshy islands. We merely stopped to purchase some food and two beaver skins, and then proceeded. Opposite to these islands the hills on the left retire, and the river widens into a kind of bay crowded with low islands, subject to be overflowed occasionally by the tide. We had not gone far from the village when the fog cleared off, and we enjoyed the delightful prospect of the ocean; that ocean, the object of all our labours, the reward of all our anxieties.

—Meriwether Lewis, *The Lewis and Clark Expedition*

On April 10, 1851, John and Sarah (Boren) Denny; their six-week-old daughter, Loretta; John's sons, Arthur, James, Samuel, Wiley, and David; Sarah's Boren children, Carson, Mary, and Louisa; Carson Boren's wife and daughter; and the two daughters of the marriage of Arthur Denny and Mary Boren left Cherry Grove, Illinois, for Oregon. A very tidy family unit, made even tidier by the later marriage of David Denny and Louisa Boren (who became known as the Sweetbriar Bride for the plants she carried from her native Illinois to the Puget Sound country) in Seattle's first and most famous wedding.

According to family legend, it was the not quite 29-year-old Arthur who was the driving force behind the family move and the prime, if not the only, reason that they arrived at Portland, Oregon, relatively intact on August 22, 1851—134 days out of Cherry Grove.

By the time they reached Portland, Arthur and his nine-months' pregnant wife Mary (Rolland Denny was born on September 2, 1851) were sick and shaking with the ague and temporarily unable to travel farther. So young David Denny and John Low, a member of another wagon party the Dennys had encountered on the trail, set out for the north on September 10 to find winter grazing for Low's cattle and, much more importantly, to explore the Puget Sound country. They walked two hundred miles to the town of Olympia. There they met Lee Terry, a young New Yorker hungry for the wilds—but malleable wilds where he could easily build his own new and better New York. These three, by boat, canoe, and foot came upon Alki Point (Terry dubbed it "New York"), which was to become the Dennys' jumping-off point for Seattle.

Alki, now as then, lies in a spectacular geographic position. On a head of land at the mouth of the Duwamish River, with a sloping sandy beach in front of a massive stand of timber (in 1851), the Cascade Mountains (and today Seattle) across a bay to the east, and the Olympic Mountains and the Peninsulas across the Sound to the west, it gives, even to this day, the illusion of being the logical stopping place for Puget Sound traffic. The only real problem with Alki, as Arthur Denny was to discover, is that it has no natural harbor.

Either David Denny, John Low, and Lee Terry weren't aware of future moorage problems, or they were so stunned by the view that they didn't care. Either way, when Low turned around to go back to Portland he was carrying a letter from David to his brother Arthur telling the rest of the Denny party to "come at once."

With Low gone, Terry and Denny worked together making preparations for the settlement until the latter part of

October when Terry managed to hitch a ride to find a frow to split cedar shakes with, and left David Denny alone.

He was alone, except for Indians and animals, for three weeks, during which time he lost his provisions, cut his foot, got sick, and ended up sitting roofless in the dark rain waiting for his family.

On November 13, 1851, the schooner *Exact* rounded the point and deposited the Denny party on the beach at Alki. The composition of the party had changed during the time since David Denny started walking north. Absent were John, Sarah, Loretta, James, Samuel, and Wiley Denny, who had opted for the relatively civilized calm of the Willamette Valley, and new additions were the Lows, the William Bell family, and Charles Terry, Lee's brother.

As it appears on a monument at Alki, the roster read:

ADULTS

Arthur A. Denny and wife	Louisa Boren
John N. Low and wife	David T. Denny
Carson D. Boren and wife	Charles C. Terry
William N. Bell and wife	Lee Terry

CHILDREN

Louisa C. Denny	Minerva Low
Lenora Denny	Gertrude Boren
Rolland H. Denny	Laura Bell
Alonzo Low	Olive Bell
Mary Low	Virginia Bell
John Low	Lavinia Bell

These, except the wandering Lee Terry, were the hardy pioneers David Denny limped down the beach to greet. These were the builders of Seattle. Only Mr. Low and Mr. Bell were over thirty.

They may have been young but they had very firm ideas of what they were about. They were not farmers, nor were they fishermen or lumberjacks. They were not afraid of work, but they knew that the work they were meant to do was work of the mind, not of the hands. They were young capitalists, young bosses in search of a labor force; people with ideas who needed bodies to bring their ideas to life. They, particularly Arthur Denny, wanted a city, not a community. To accomplish this, it was necessary for them to do some very strange, unpioneerlike things.

First of all, Arthur Denny decided they had to move the site of their city-to-be. Alki was lovely, but impractical. Ships could not dock there. Arthur Denny, Bell, and Boren paddled all about Elliott Bay taking soundings with a clothesline until they found a spot with what they hoped was enough depth. Then, on February 15, 1852, they staked claims on land across the bay and slightly north of Alki. Those claims were to be the foundation of the city of Seattle.

Once they had chosen a location, they needed men to work on it.

Murray Morgan describes the first of these "needed men" in *Skid Road*:

> In 1850 Dr. David Swinson Maynard was living in Lorain County, Ohio; he was forty-two years old and in debt. On the morning of April 9 he shook hands with his wife Lydia, whom in twenty years of marriage he had come to dislike, kissed his two children, mounted his gray mule, and rode off toward California, where he hoped to recoup his fortunes. Maynard intended to join another Ohioan, Colonel John B. Weller, in the gold fields, but kindness and cholera sidetracked him. Instead of panning for nuggets he became one of the founding fathers of Seattle and in some ways the most influential figure of the early days on Elliott Bay.

On his way to the gold fields, Maynard stopped to give medical assistance to a wagon train afflicted with cholera. One of the members of the train party, a man named Broshears, died and Maynard left his own California-bound party to help the man's widow reach her brother who had settled at Tumwater on the extreme southern tip of Puget Sound. Maynard fell in love with the widow and, when he delivered her to her destination, he fell in love with the Pacific Northwest. California's gold was gone for him forever. He felled and sold trees until he had enough money to buy stock for outfitting a trading post/store, and then with his new-found friend Sealth, chief of the Duwamish, he headed north and offered his services and his enterprise to the Alki/New York settlers in exchange for a partnership in their would-be city. The Dennys were ready to move across the bay to their new site, and they convinced Maynard that he would be better off with their harbor than on the windy beach of Alki. On May 23, 1853, the official platting of the new town listed Maynard, Arthur Denny, and Boren as equal partners, and they took the name of Maynard's friend, the old Chief Sealth, for that of the city.

Maynard traded with the Indians and hired them to cure and pack salmon (which tended to spoil in shipment to San Francisco) and cut down trees for lumber. He served as doctor, justice of the peace, and as a community social director. Most importantly, he was Seattle's first, most personable, and least selfish public booster.

Maynard agreed with Arthur Denny that the future of the city was, or should be, every resident's first concern. But, unlike Denny—who held on to what he owned—Maynard was willing to take risks with what he had, to give away things like land, trusting that his generosity would be remembered.

Henry Yesler was forty-two years old when he arrived in Seattle in 1852. Two years younger than Dr. Maynard, he seemed an elder statesman to the other founding fathers, whose average age was twenty-six. Not only was he an older, whittling, taciturn, self-serving man; he had capital. More precisely, he had the guaranteed financial backing to build a steam sawmill after he had found the "ideal" location—something he was more than happy to point out.

Murray Morgan describes Yesler's arrival and Maynard's reaction:

> This was the Yesler whom Maynard's friend, Colonel John Weller, had said intended to start a sawmill "somewhere in Oregon." Now here he was, hunting a site. He had inspected New York–Alki across the bay and found it promising. Of course, this side of the bay looked good too, but the best land on this side was taken. The ideal place for a mill would be right on the spit, where Maynard had set the Indians to salting salmon. The spit had level ground with deep water alongside, but this was Maynard's property and Boren's, and they had already done some clearing. Of course they wouldn't want to give up cleared land; that was understandable. Well, it was a pleasure to have met them and he wished the town well. Yesler strode back toward his dugout to return to Alki for another look. Maynard and Boren went into a quick conference.
>
> A mill meant jobs for the citizens. It meant regular calls by the lumber ships, and that in turn meant the population would grow. A mill meant the land would be cleared rapidly. Property values would rise. No other town on the Sound had a steam mill. . . . The town that got Yesler's steam mill would have a toehold on the future. There was only one thing to do, and Maynard and Boren did it. They told Yesler he could have the strip of waterfront where the Maynard and Boren claims joined.

Yesler agreed and Seattle got the mill. Again the stakes were lifted and the claim sites marked off anew. Maynard made the biggest sacrifice, giving up the best section of his waterfront.

This was in 1852. By March, 1853, Yesler's mill was not only operating, but was doing about three thousand dollars worth of business each week. Maynard had made his sacrifice and done his public relations work, Yesler was on his way to his fortune, and Seattle was beginning to realize her future.

Less than a year and a half after David Denny's dark, miserable greeting of his family on the beach at Alki, Seattle had the elements necessary to start Arthur Denny's city. Of the young pioneer/capitalists who comprised the Denny party, Arthur was really the only survivor. Bell and Boren, the Terrys, and Low all but faded away. David worked for the land he loved, but the city broke him and he died poor, as the civically sentimental "last pioneer," in 1903. David Maynard gave his energy, charm, and openhearted dreams. And Henry Yesler showed Arthur Denny a grown-up capitalist in action.

It was those four men—Arthur and David Denny, David Maynard, and Henry Yesler—who held the seeds of what was to become Seattle. The two brothers: Arthur, who felt that the land was his through the divine right of discovery, his to keep or deal away as he saw fit, and his the power to pick the dwellers on the land; and David, who felt he was the land's temporary tenant. And the two newcomers, invited residents: Maynard and Yesler, older men of the world, experienced in the ways of life, one in the giving and the other in the taking.

The opening of Yesler's mill is a good place to stop in recounting the chronological history of Seattle. Before the sawmill, any work in the infant town had been either necessary for the physical survival of the community or, as in Maynard's experiment with the Indian-packed salmon or the amateur cutting of pilings, an attempt to find an industrial direction. The mill brought real and permanent industry and with it Seattle's first labor force. It marked the beginning of resident hired help.

The idea of Seattle became reality.

Arthur Denny
and the Seattle Spirit

> He was kindly and he was stern for the right. It was largely due to his high and even strict standards that Seattle arose from being an obscure sawmill town located "at the mouth of the Duwamish" to what it is today, a world city. From the very start he planned it to be a great seaport;—he had the vision and the engineer's mind to know that it had those possibilities. For years he fought tenaciously and from every angle for a wagon road over the Cascades. He realized that until Seattle had some way of exit she was destined to remain obscure.
>
> —Clarence B. Bagley, *History of King County, Washington* (1929)

> The most important thing in my estimation is to make no wrong or incorrect statements. Let it be the pride of old settlers to state the truth. It is no time for romancing or painting fancy sketches when we are nearing the end of our voyage. The work is too serious for fiction. We want solid facts only.
>
> —Arthur A. Denny, *Pioneer Days on Puget Sound* (1888)

Arthur Denny, twenty-nine years old when he founded the city of Seattle, remains to this day an enigma. To William Speidel, he was "Our Father," the second, if not the first (behind Chief Sealth), of the *Sons of the Profits*, those heroic souls who started a virgin wilderness along the road to becoming a commercial conglomerate.

Arthur Denny was Roberta Frye Watt's grandfather, and she paints a very different picture of him than does Speidel. In her book *Four Wagons West*, Denny comes out better than Odysseus. Even with the ague, shivering one day and boiling the next, he set out from Portland, Oregon, on the schooner *Exact*, captained by Isaiah Folger from the island of Nantucket, and when they landed at Alki Point, he took charge.

His brother David—deserted first by Low and then by Terry, sick as a dog with his pathetic gimped-up foot, no roof over his head, Indians and animals his only company —probably told them to get the hell out of there. But Arthur, still sick, dropped the crying women and the wet, stupefied children onto the beach, and set about to build houses. First a roof for the house that David was supposed to have finished, then one for himself, then one for Boren.

A tough, hard, big man. Much bigger than the squat, stooped-over Indians he confronted; a man one had to respect. Seattle's first realtor.

It may be hard for anyone who is not a businessman to appreciate Arthur Denny's innate business sense. The Denny party did not leave Illinois because they were broke or persecuted; they weren't Mormons or Pilgrims. They set out because of reports of opportunities in the West and because the winter was lousy in Cherry Grove, Illinois. So, at least according to his granddaughter, Arthur Denny said, "Mary, will you go?"

They went.

It was a business venture.

They left Cherry Grove on April 10, 1851, and on December 10, 1851, they were in business. The brig *Leonesa* came around Alki Point and asked for pilings, and the Denny party cut down the immediate trees all around and gave them to her.

Soon Arthur Denny realized that the winter storms made the loading of the pilings impossible, nor was there even enough timber available on Alki to satisfy the demand. He decided that his city had to be someplace else. Setting out with a clothesline and horseshoes to find a channel with the right depth, he fastened on to land with enough wood to turn a profit. He had found the place.

So much for Alki, so much more for Seattle.

Arthur Denny didn't stop with building houses or cutting pilings. He was hell-bent to build an empire, and if he wasn't as slick as Jim Hill, the empire builder himself, he was just as determined. He wanted a city, a state, and a fortune.

He had no use for dawdlers or those who wanted to work only eight hours a day. He had no truck with tobacco or liquor, or with Indians for that matter, unless it was profitable to use them.

Speidel is right when he talks about profit as the moving force in the founding of Seattle. Certainly Arthur Denny wanted money more than anything else, but at that stage in America's history, who didn't? Land was something to be *owned*. The trip of the Denny party from Cherry Grove to what was to become Seattle was no pleasant one-day outing; it was a forced march toward what Arthur Denny knew must be theirs.

It must have been horrible, despite the saccharine that history has spilled over it. But they couldn't stop. And one wonders, was it Arthur Denny who drove them? His diary of the trip West is certainly dry enough, self-contained, as the man himself must have been. There is no wonder or amazement in Arthur Denny's diary. It suggests what a passenger aboard a transcontinental 747 might write today: "Down the Platte. Crossed the Missouri."

Except that they had no comfort, no stewardesses, and no movies. Instead, they had their four wagons, until they met up with the Low party, and they had fear.

Fear is something that Arthur Denny and most of those who came after him never wanted to talk about. They would rather talk about bravery and strength, their conscious virtues. But there is no element of awe in praising strength; there is in recognizing fear. And fear is what most of them must have felt.

The fear of strangeness. Not just the Indians, but the flatlands, the mountains, the sea beyond. Most of all, the fear that none of them, save maybe Arthur Denny, knew where they were going, or why.

So in reading accounts of the opening of the Northwest, the only things you encounter are dry yet sentimental stories of bravery and conquest. Emotions are closed off by time, and the pain is looked back upon with chuckles.

We are taught that America was a virgin wilderness which had to be tamed, whipped the way a bad jockey whips a bad horse to make it finish in the money. We are taught that it is courageous to conquer, cowardly to stay put. It's no wonder that Arthur Denny, having dragged his family from their homes to what was then the edge of the world, had to stand bold and tall, sick or not, and be courageous.

Arthur Denny was good; God grant him that. He wanted to bring religion to his city and I'm sure was terribly disappointed when the prayer meetings consisted of himself, his wife, and the preacher and his wife. He wanted vice out of his city. Church-going, clean, nice people. He would take care of the Indians.

He tried his damnedest.

He never liked them, nobody except Dr. Maynard and David Denny did, but Arthur Denny tried to deal with them. He excused their smell, their dumbness, even their curiosity, yet for some reason they never really excused him. They never trusted him. David Denny, yes; but not Arthur Denny. It was again the profit motive. They knew he wanted the land, which was not theirs, but with which they lived in peace and balance, and Arthur Denny set about with stern-minded willfulness not only to own the land, but to change it, to make it suitable and profitable for the white population of his city. To the Indians, this was heresy. The various tribes of the Northwest fought, but it was not for outright ownership of the land; they had never heard of Manifest Destiny.

And that was Arthur Denny's Bible.

When Henry Yesler arrived, Arthur Denny's experiment with the clothesline and horseshoes proved to be as sound as Ben Franklin's famous kite-flying. Yesler wanted land for a sawmill. Seattle gave it to him and built him a slide to get the timber down to the waterfront mill; Arthur Denny's city was in business. The water was deep enough for boats to get right up to the mill dock; the slide performed beautifully, and everybody worked twelve hours a day.

Arthur Denny went to the legislature and became a powerful territorial and, later, state figure, but his first and abiding love and concern was for his city. He built it and it seemed, for a time at least, that he decided who could and who could not live there.

He hated interference and condescension, especially from outside the city limits. Yet he knew he had to build, or the city of his dreams would be nothing but a piddling little logging town. So, when the Reverend Daniel Bagley arrived, Arthur Denny came as close as he ever would to being "taken." He was already wheeling and dealing his way through his seventh term in the legislature, managing to get the rights to a university for Seattle and whittling the stipulation of 160 gift acres by the townspeople down to 10. It was the Reverend Bagley who called his bluff. Reverend Bagley wanted to build a church (he had twenty to his credit at the time) but Seattle already had one, so he settled for the university, and he conned Arthur Denny into giving him eight and a third acres of Denny's land, Lee Terry and Edward Lander the rest of the required ten, and on May 20, 1861, the cornerstone of Seattle's university was laid.

Arthur Denny knew that Seattleites could not live by the sea alone. Indian settlements could, but not a city. There had to be a way, other than shipping, to cart the beauties of the wilderness to the rest of America, and to bring back the money. But the mountains were in the way. A virgin, like Arthur Denny's Seattle, does not bestow her bounties on a carnal house like San Francisco. The mountains had to be conquered, and the railroad was the way to do it.

The landing of that plum was to be the destiny of the feisty little Irishman Thomas Burke, who with Jim Hill's money, trust, and power in his pocket would bring the Great Northern into Seattle, break the Northern Pacific, and put the silver bullet into Tacoma's heart.

Arthur Denny never knew that. History has a way of fooling those who play with it. What he wanted was to reach Walla Walla; from there it would be easy. America would be open to what Seattle, and Seattle alone, would offer the less fortunate who had made the mistake of stopping in Iowa. Timber, fish, God knew what else.

But the trains had to be there. Arthur Denny knew full well the increasingly awesome power of San Francisco, and the potential threat of that settlement down south, Tacoma. He trekked out into the mountains, trusting, as he did occasionally, the judgment and knowledge of the Indians, to find his passage East, for himself and for his city.

Although Denny's railroad never made it to Walla Walla, under the guidance of James Colman the Seattle & Walla Walla stretched twenty-two miles out to Newcastle and hauled back coal. That meant jobs, and it meant money, because the coal was shipped to a hungry San Francisco.

The S & WW would do until the empire builder arrived.

Arthur Denny and Dexter Horton. Penniless, Dexter Horton moved into Seattle to stay in the fall of 1853. He and his wife got jobs running the cookhouse for a sawmill in Port Gamble, where they remained nine months saving $1,160, and then he went to work in Henry Yesler's sawmill while his wife took charge of that cookhouse. Later he opened up a general store, in partnership with David Phillips, and came up with an unusual idea: he held the money for mill and farm hands, trappers, and loggers in little sacks with their names on them and when the number of sacks began to grow, he bought a safe. Seattle had a bank.

In 1866 Horton and Phillips sold the store, Horton going to San Francisco to try his hand at the brokerage business. In 1870 he returned to Seattle and entered into a real banking venture with Phillips (theirs was for ten years Seattle's only bank). Then, in 1872, Phillips died, and Dexter Horton had a new partner: Arthur Denny.

A booklet put out by the Dexter Horton National Bank commemorating its golden anniversary says, as quoted by Mrs. Watt: " 'Horton and Denny's bank is good enough for me' became the universal expression among men from Victoria to Olympia. From all parts of the Puget Sound country in the 70's came men to deposit their money with the confidence of Englishmen in the Bank of England."

So Arthur Denny became a banker as well as founding father, logger, realtor, and legislator: a man of many parts, able to wear many different hats.

But what sort of man walked underneath those hats? What drove him to conquer piece after disparate piece in the tiny, but constantly expanding, world he had created in an awesome virgin wilderness?

Arthur Denny thought of himself as a capitalist. In America today, that word has bad, dollar-hungry connotations, and few would so baldly and proudly profess themselves capitalists, as they did in early Seattle guidebooks.

But in America's youth, which lasted until the continent was covered and subdued, capitalists were only laborers with the cunning ability to keep their money and use it to make more money.

It wasn't a matter of simple greed. Men like Arthur Denny were driven by a desire for dignity and respect—and a curious type of religious fervor.

He was sincere. He never smoked, drank, or swore. He even blew the whistle on Doc Maynard's irritating habits. He tried to bring the City of God to earth, to make his Seattle the New Jerusalem, but the dollar kept getting in the way. Everywhere he turned there was money to be made, and not necessarily in the service of the Lord.

And maybe not in the best service of his family. Whether people want to talk about it or not, something very bad happened in 1893, when David Denny, broke, turned his back on Seattle and walked off into the woods. As his daughter, Emily Inez Denny, says in her book, *Blazing the Way:*

> Mr. Denny was once, not so very long ago, a wealthy man—some say the wealthiest in the city—but he died poor, very poor; but he paid his debts to the full. Once the owner in fee simple of land upon which are now a thousand beautiful Seattle homes, he passed on to his account a stranger in a strange land and without title to his own domicile. . . .
>
> The Deficiency Judgment and renewal of the same gives opportunity for greedy and unprincipled creditors to rob the debtor. There should be a law compelling the return of the surplus. When one class of people make many times their money out of the misfortunes of others, there is manifestly great inequality.
>
> The principles of some are to grab all they can, "skin" all they can, and follow up all they can even to the *graveyard.*

Angry daughter? The making of a radical? Or, maybe simply so furious at her Uncle Arthur that she couldn't put it down in print; it was, after all, Dexter Horton and Arthur Denny's bank that foreclosed on David Denny. As Emily Inez says, in all caps:

THESE THINGS OUGHT NOT SO TO BE.

Compare Emily Denny's "manifestly great inequality" with "the Seattle Spirit" and you get some strange results. The eloquence of certain writers speaks to the point. First, L. Byrd Mock, in *The Seattle Spirit,* published in 1911:

> This [we-are-going-to-win-out] dominant characteristic of Seattle people has given rise to the concrete term "Seattle Spirit," an expression coined nearly twenty years ago, to portray that tremendous psychic that seems to exist, carrying everything before it, a transforming agent that molds things to the heart's desire. It is a combination of energy, determination, and optimism—a trait that has made Seattle famous. Many definitions of this potent force have been given, one of the best being that of Hon. Richard A. Ballinger, former secretary of the interior, who says: "The Seattle Spirit is the expression of the high tide of American genius and enterprise in the social and commercial activities of the day."

Frightening, but Mock lived at high tide, and everything in Seattle was peaches and cream to him.

Carl W. Art and R. A. Wegner published in 1930 a book titled *Seattle: World City That Had to Be* with the Metropolitan Press in Seattle. Miscellanies from their text:

> . . . the authors, comparative newcomers in this city of newcomers, this "generation city," began informing themselves about its history and discovered . . . romance!

Recent, pulsing romance in word and picture. . . . What made it the largest city of its age in the world?

Was it magic? Or just a combination of rich resources, congenial climate, unlimited harbor possibilities, strategic position, and the refusal of a courageous people to admit their limitations and be halted by the obstacles imposed by warring Indians, a tardy government, and by nature itself. . . . It can't be done, doesn't apply in Seattle. The whole city is a Monument witnessing the fact that it CAN! . . .

In this most beautiful setting, America's *ideal* city is being brought to maturity.

Everything modern—metropolitan. No slums or narrow business streets. Planned and zoned, not just haphazard accident. [Evidently Art and Wegner were unaware of the botch-up in the initial platting of the city. Maynard laid out the streets one way; Arthur Denny and Boren another. They couldn't reach a compromise so they just left the streets running into each other. So much for city planning.] More education, less illiteracy. Better health, better homes, happy homeowning, native-born Americans. That's Seattle! One of the country's cleanest, most picturesque cities by day. One of the most artistic and brilliantly lighted by night. . . .

It is ultra-modern—neither wild nor woolly. How could it be otherwise? Eighty-three percent of its population is native American, and ninety-seven percent speak and read English.

. . . her people having been recruited from sterling stock, time, thought and money have been given unstintedly to transplant here the culture of other sections.

In the eyes of Mock, Art, and Wegner, Seattle had become even more than Arthur Denny could have dreamed.

On July 30, 1903 (eight years before Mock published his book), the Spirit had its day. Called Semi-Centennial Celebration of the Founding of Seattle under auspices of the

Chamber of Commerce, the day consisted of a morning parade and afternoon and evening speeches punctuated by a formal dinner. Everything that happened was focused on trying to pin down and identify once and for all that elusive "spirit." Even some of the remaining Indians, called First Pioneers, were rounded up, befeathered, and forced into the parade.

Excerpts from just two of the day's speeches stand as a testament to the feelings of the Chamber of Commerce and, it was hoped, the people. The afternoon session was called to order and addressed by Colonel William F. Prosser, the chairman of the Chamber committee in charge of the celebration. He said, in part:

> Christopher Columbus may have regretted his discovery of America, because it interfered with his proposed voyage to the East Indies, but the founders of Seattle never wished to look further for a location for one of the world's great emporiums of commerce. . . . If the high ideals of truth and honor, of progress, industry and enterprise which were cherished by the founders of Seattle shall be maintained by their descendants, then indeed they will show themselves worthy of the magnificent heritage which they now possess.

The evening ceremonies were keynoted by James B. Meikle, secretary of the Chamber of Commerce, who said:

> Back of all these resources we have the indomitable "Seattle spirit." That is the spirit that takes hold of every one who becomes a resident of this city and inspires him with energy, enterprise and enthusiasm. It opens his eyes and makes him see the glorious possibilities of this matchless country. It stimulates his faculties and makes him fearless in his business enterprises, confident of his success, dauntless in the face of dangers and difficulties

and strong when standing for his rights. . . . It came here fifty-one years ago with Arthur A. Denny and his associates; it has been here ever since, and it will be here until the City of Seattle has everything the heart of man can desire.

But in spite of the "vision" of Arthur Denny and the fervent hopes of men like Meikle, Seattle did not get "everything the heart of man can desire." Maybe that was because Denny got his piety mixed up with a vigorous survival-of-the-fittest code and those who followed eliminated the piety. Seattle was never meant to be a religious town, something that Arthur Denny could not see. By the time he founded his city, America was too far down the road of commercialism to be bothered lifting its eyes heavenward. There were too many things to be done and those "happy homeowning, native-born Americans" who got there first reaped the profits, while the dawdlers and the foreign-born got nothing but the back of the communal hand.

The Seattle Spirit. Its soft, sweet blanket covers only achievers; the rest do not belong.

Yet people hate to leave Seattle. Even driven out, they look back wistfully at what might have been. Maybe it was only David Denny who was able to turn his back completely on his brother's city. David Denny—and the Chinese laborers who realized, while being escorted to the boat, that once the tracks for the railroad were laid Seattle was not their Manifest Destiny.

Boats, Trains, and Planes

Well, I am going to read you something from Theodore Roosevelt
and this says it better than I could ever hope to say it. My
philosophy of life. This is not to say I don't love pleasures of life. I
do. It is not to say that I don't have compassion for those who are
unfortunate. I do. This is the way I feel about my own life: "It is
not the critic who counts, not the man who points out how the
strong man stumbles or where the doer of deeds could have done
them better. The credit belongs to the man who is actually in the
arena, whose face is marked by dust and sweat and blood, who
strives valiantly, who errs and comes up short again and again, who
knows the great enthusiasms, the great devotions and spends
himself in a worthy cause. Who at the best knows in the end the
triumphs of high achievements and who at the worst, if he fails, at
least fails while daring greatly so that his place will never be with
those cold and timid souls who know neither defeat nor victory."

—from an interview with William Allen, lawyer,
president, chairman of the board, the Boeing Company

In his book, *He Built Seattle,* Robert C. Nesbit says, "The
Denny-Terry party that selected the site [of Seattle] was
not a group of land-seeking farmers but urban pioneers
determined to found a future city." "Urban pioneers"
has a frighteningly too familiar sound for late twentieth-
century ears. The word urban qualifies and defines our
failures and diseases, from squalor to madness, and it seems
that only a lunatic would set out to be a pioneer of cities.

But to a young man in America in the 1850s, a city in the
wilderness was something to create, a dream, not an op-
pressive nightmare. The borders of the continent had been
established by the physical presence of Americans. That
which still seemed strange, wild, and dangerous would not
remain so for long. Arthur Denny and others like him

realized this when they looked at the land. These urban pioneers were not misfits, unwashed and unwanted immigrants desperately grabbing at enough free government land to protect themselves and their families from a hostile society. On the contrary, they saw themselves as solid native-born Americans, suffering only in the fact that they were country people instead of being rich, cultured, and respected New Yorkers or Bostonians. The conquering of the continent, the opening of the land and the wild-eyed, this-land-is-our-land optimistic fervor of Manifest Destiny, offered very real possibilities to the young of Ohio and Illinois, the opportunity for clerks and surveyors to become genuine capitalists. If they could not be New Yorkers in New York, they would build their own new and better New Yorks.

Building a New York, though, is considerably more complicated than clearing and staking the acreage for a farm. A city builder does not clear the land in order to cultivate it. He has no intention of living off his land or with it. Land is his financial base, his starting point, his collateral. And, as it is the farmer's need to protect his land from neighbors, it is the city builder's need to allow access to his property, or at least to his dream for the future. He *needs* neighbors, familiar or strange. He must constantly sell his ideas and hold fast to the control of what he wants to build. Arthur Denny was not out to build art museums and universities; he wanted history to remember him for establishing a place with a sound economic foundation and reputation—a city that would last, grow, and be respected.

Arthur Denny, or someone with Denny's determination, was probably the only type of white mid-nineteenth-century American who could have survived the Puget Sound country. The alternative to a Denny would have been a white man who would simply have replaced the Indian, living quietly and communally with the sea and the land.

It was not an area for commercial farming or ranching; the severity of the terrain, enclosed by mountains and the water, did not offer a settler room to expand. One could not possess, control, or cultivate enough to become wealthy. Living like an Indian was unthinkable for a man who wanted more, not less, civilization, and that meant the only way open for a settler was to build a city, a commercial center.

On December 10, 1851, the little group of settlers comprising the Denny party found out they had a saleable product right behind their campsite on the beach at Alki Point.

The brig *Leonesa*, searching for lumber to rebuild the burned-out piers of San Francisco, anchored off the Point and the captain asked Arthur Denny if the camp had any pilings for sale. It did not take the settlers very long to figure out what pilings were or to cut down the trees to supply them. Resident capitalism was born in the Pacific Northwest.

It was the arrival of the *Leonesa* that sent Arthur Denny across Elliott Bay in a canoe carrying a clothesline and horseshoes for depth soundings in search of a better site for his city with deeper water for a natural harbor. And it was the arrival of the *Leonesa* that made the settlers so ready to greet Henry Yesler and his "guaranteed" steam sawmill.

It was also, perversely perhaps, the presence of the *Leonesa*, representing the demands of San Francisco and the infant camp's attempt to meet those demands with supplies, that propelled New York/Alki/Seattle into a crazed obsession with transportation, an obsession that continues to this very day and whose result has been an enormity of power and control over a major American city by a single corporation—the Boeing Company.

For a fledgling farmer, maybe, filling the hold of the *Leonesa* and other ships like her every few months with felled trees might be enough. Enough at least for some extra molasses, real tea, and a jug or two of store-bought spirits. But for would-be city builders it would not do to serve as handmaiden for another city. The idea from the beginning was to protect the producer from ever having to sit on the dock waiting for somebody else's ship to come for his goods. Seattle would not be subject to anyone else's whims. It would be the city to which the ships, or whatever vehicle, had to come—or, better yet, the city from which the vehicles came.

This was a heady notion. Seattle could not be New York, the clearinghouse for America's new citizens from Europe and the point of contact between America and the rest of the civilized world. Nor could it hope to replace Chicago, already solidly squatting across America's heartland. With her limited marketable products (lumber, minerals, fish) and her access to a desirable Far Eastern market unknown, there was a grave possibility from the start that the most Seattle might hope for was status as a major post office.

In order to avoid being merely a clearinghouse for California markets and supplying San Francisco with lumber and coal, the early residents of Seattle knew they must have their own route to the American East. If San Francisco, at least temporarily, controlled shipping by sea, then Seattle would go by land—through the mountains and across the plains. That meant the railroad. Even in the 1850s Northwest settlers knew that in a very short time the continent would be united by a northern rail line (one of the theories for explaining the furious speed with which the Indian treaties of the fifties were concluded was that the land simply had to be cleared for the rights of way). What they did not know was where that railroad would plant its western terminus. For that, ambitious Seattleites had to prepare themselves and then wait, court and be courted, pretty themselves up for prospective lover/investors, compete and be rejected. It seemed an unbearably slow and bleak process. There was always the possibility of losing out to Portland—older, larger, and with an enviable river route east. Or to Tacoma or Bellingham with their promises of easier access routes and more control for the prospective investor. The Northern Pacific railroad seemed to taunt and tease Seattle with the threat of trunkline status. But the Northern Pacific alternated between failure and discredita- tion. And Seattle held fast with its hole card—its incredible natural harbor, the result of Arthur Denny's clothesline soundings.

Seattle grew slowly in its first twenty-five years, func- tioning as a way station between the California markets and the harvestable natural bounty of the Northwest. By 1875 it was little more than a mill town and marketplace of three thousand people.

In 1890, there were 42,000 inhabitants in Seattle, by 1900, 80,671, and, in 1910, 237,194. Edwin J. Cohn, Jr., a puzzled economist, tried to explain what happened to Seattle in his book, *Industry in the Pacific Northwest and the Location Theory:*

> The growth of Seattle is far more difficult to account for [than Portland's]. An important seaport, it lacks a river and easy access to the interior. It is, in fact, cut off from the interior by the Cascade Range, which all traffic must surmount. Less favorably situated than Portland and founded later, Seattle has become bigger and more im- portant. How has this happened? From its founding in 1852 as the first settlement of Puget Sound, Seattle grew steadily as a sawmill town until the Alaska gold rush. . . . There seems to have been no particular geographic reason why Seattle should have developed rather than Tacoma, or even Everett or Bellingham to the north. All started around sawmills, cutting the trees which, in the nineteenth century, grew down to the water's edge. In 1890 Tacoma was almost as large a city as Seattle and the western terminus of the Northern Pacific Railroad. The

best explanation of Seattle's capture of the Alaska trade
and consequent spectacular growth is that a few of its
citizens were particularly aggressive and imaginative.
The other towns were too busy making money out of the
lumber business to be bothered with Alaska.

On June 6, 1889, a fire destroyed sixty-five blocks of
downtown Seattle—almost the entire business district. Instead of recoiling with despair, Seattleites set about re-
building, putting brick, iron, and stone where there had
been wooden structures. The fire cleaned up the town for
the residents. Most citizens of means probably agreed with
Judge Thomas Burke, businessman, speculator, and lawyer
for the Great Northern railway, when he said:

> While the fire was perhaps the most disastrous that ever
> occurred on the Pacific Coast, it was not an unmixed evil.
> Inside of eighteen months we shall have probably the
> best built City of its size in the Country. The new Seattle
> will be in all respects vastly superior to the old. No doubt
> individuals have suffered greatly—some of them being
> ruined by this terrible disaster—but the City will bear no
> trace of it in eighteen months. There is already more
> capital here from the East than we ever have had before.
> The fire had scarcely been extinguished before the re-
> building of the City and the re-establishment of business
> in the various lines had been begun. The vigor and en-
> ergy displayed at home inspired confidence abroad. The
> result is, that money for investment here has flowed in
> in great streams, and the Banks have now on deposit
> more than they ever had before. [July 1, 1889.]

The fire gave currency to the term "Seattle Spirit."
Whether you take Cohn saying "a few of its citizens were
particularly aggressive and imaginative," or Burke with his
"vigor and energy," you come up with the same thing: the

ability of Seattle's people in power to be calm, canny, and productive in the face of adversity.

The names are unimportant. They changed—from Arthur Denny to Thomas Burke to William Allen—all really the same person wearing different fashions. What is important is the attitude that the establishment of businessmen, lawyers, bankers, realtors, and labor leaders impressed upon the townspeople—that Seattle would become a city if its citizens stayed home.

In 1893 Seattle got its railroad when the Great Northern established its western terminus in the city. It was a much better deal than fighting with the Northern Pacific, which demanded ownership of the timberland, because Jim Hill was a railroad baron—he wanted his road, not the land (although Hill and his friend Frederick Weyerhaeuser were certainly not against owning the lumber the railroad shipped). Seattle got its way East without being dependent upon Tacoma, Portland, or any other coastal city.

In 1897 the gold rush hit the Yukon, and Seattle, despite the anguished cries of San Francisco, became the port for Alaska. On July 17, 1897, when the steamer *Portland* arrived in Seattle from Alaska, local publicists let it be known that Seattle had "a ton of gold" and started a rush of humanity to and through Seattle. Wise Seattleites stayed home, transporting and servicing. Seattle was now established as a primary port, one that could manufacture its own ships with the surety that they would be used because local business interests needed them. With its transportation links to the rest of America secured by rail, its control of Alaskan shipping, and the opening (in 1914) of the Panama Canal, Seattle could begin to think of itself as central to the economy of the country, yet still a city fiercely proud of its independence.

There was no need to exhaust the resources of the region by shipping out all of its goods. The city's experience in tying itself commercially to the continent made those in control very aware that the means of transportation were every bit as important as what was carried. Shipbuilding therefore was a natural, and most Seattle businessmen and industrialists saw the future tied to the sea—through *Seattle's* port and *Seattle's* ships.

There was one wealthy resident, however, who thought otherwise.

In January, 1910, a few miles south of Los Angeles, William Boeing attended the first international flying meet to be held in the United States. He liked what he saw.

Boeing was young. His family had built a large fortune from iron ore and timber in Minnesota, and, raised by a strict, education-conscious mother (his father died when William was eight), Boeing had gone to boarding school in America and Switzerland and to the Sheffield Scientific School at Yale. In 1903, a year shy of graduation and twenty-two years old, Boeing took his inheritance and used it to make his own fortune in the timber of the Pacific Northwest.

Boeing was an accepted and respected member of the monied elite in Seattle, but when he talked about his dreams of the fun and profit to be found in flying, he was teased, if not openly ridiculed. Henry Broderick describes one evening of Boeing-baiting in his book, *The "HB" Story:*

> On a Saturday night at the University Club in October of 1913 was held a gay gathering following the Harvard-Yale football game. The banter was bouncy and bon hommie of college guys. . . .
>
> A young man named Bill Boeing was one of the more restrained members of the party. He and Conrad Westervelt were building a seaplane out on Lake Union in a small shed bordering on the water. Bill Boeing was the scion of a family richly endowed in the world's goods,

and in his own right was the possessor of a rather formi-
dable fortune. He was also the possessor of a mentality
with a mission.

This was a time when the average man was apt to look
askance at anyone interested in aircraft. The school
books had dealt humorously with "Darius Green And
His Flying Machine" and that just about settled the matter in the mind of the Man In The Street.

. . . on that evening at the University Club, Bill Boeing
was the target for many a jibe tossed at him by the con-
vivial celebrants. One of the more caustic of the critics,
insinuating that Bill might presently be in need of a
guardian, or that his cranium was full of canaries, got a
reply to his corny cliches. Bill declared, with some acid
in his tones, that most of those present would live to see
planes arriving and departing from Airports, precisely as
trains came and went from Railroad Stations. This was
too much of a strain on the credulity or imagination of
the group, and to a man, they indulged in a Gargantuan
guffaw!

Initially Bill Boeing may have just wanted to build a
plane for his own amusement (in much the same spirit he
had shown in buying the Heath shipyard to finish building
a yacht). But conversations both fanciful and serious with
Conrad Westervelt, a naval engineer, fellow bachelor, and
alumnus of the Sheffield School, culminated in trial flights
over Lake Washington in a Curtiss-type hydroplane piloted
by Terah Maroney on July 4, 1914, and notions of personal
pleasure were turned into purely secondary concerns.

Boeing and Westervelt went into business, experimen-
tally at first, building trial planes they called B & W's, and
then, on July 15, 1916, William Boeing had his lawyers draw
up articles of incorporation. He had twenty-one workers.

In 1916, only a madman or a rich visionary would have
incorporated an airplane factory in Seattle. Seattle ship-

building had been growing rapidly since the gold rush and on September 7, 1916, the United States Congress passed legislation creating the United States Shipping Board and its subsidiary, the Emergency Fleet Corporation. In *The Seattle General Strike,* Robert Friedheim describes the function of the board and the corporation:

> The Emergency Fleet Corporation . . . had a dual function—to create shipyards and ships and to supervise the use of the ships the Corporation built. The United States government, under the 1916 act creating the Board and Corporation, was neither to own nor to operate the shipyards. Although the government would own the ships, they were, in the main, to be operated by private interests. Thus one of the two main functions of the Emergency Fleet Corporation was to use government funds— originally $50,000,000, then increased to $750,000,000, and finally to $2,884,000,000—not merely to purchase ships but to provide the capital required by private interests to create the shipyards.

This was great bait for the hungry human fish of a booming port city. Seattle bit at it ravenously. Before 1914, the Seattle Dry Dock and Construction Company was alone in manufacturing steel-hulled ships in the city; by 1918 there were five steel shipyards and twelve yards manufacturing wooden-hulled ships. The unseen problem, of course, lay in the dependency of the industry on the government's need to buy ships. When the government decided, with the end of World War I, that it didn't want ships anymore, the boom went bust. And Seattle had its General Strike of 1919. But while the boom lasted, shipbuilding was *the* industry in town, and Seattle seemed to be *the* shipbuilding city in the nation. As such, she had to go out and recruit skilled labor to fill the 35,000 jobs suddenly opened by shipyard expansion, jobs which the owners had to know would not be permanent yet must be filled with workers attracted by the illusion of permanence, along with the lure of higher wages, which would cause them to leave San Francisco or Portland. It was the same problem magnified of unwanted but necessary labor that faced Denny and Yesler in the frontier sawmill days of the community, and it set a nasty precedent which would be followed with much more catastrophic results by the Boeing Company some forty years later.

For the time being, though, Bill Boeing was content to watch the shipbuilding boom and move carefully into the air. He was content to do this because he could afford to. A man who was dependent upon outside investors for his capital, whether individuals or government agencies, could never have done what Boeing did. But he paid his own bills. He controlled his industry and could do what he wanted, even down to quitting when he got mad.

As America began to realize that the future lay in air travel and transport, things went marvelously for the man and the company. In the original 1916 articles of incorporation, Boeing had his attorneys set up a company that would not only manufacture airplanes and other products, but would "act as a common carrier of passengers and freight by aerial navigation" as well. Boeing planned on his company not only building, but owning, operating, and scheduling—total control, a monopoly.

The company expanded by getting government contracts, mail runs, and, on July 1, 1927, Jane Eads, a Chicago newspaper reporter, got on a Boeing Air Transport plane in Chicago and arrived in San Francisco twenty-three hours later. The first commercial airline passenger.

Boeing Air Transport became United Airlines, a corporate cousin to the Boeing Company in a new conglomerate called United Aircraft and Transport Corporation, and William Boeing seemed to be reaching a position where he could put his competition out of business before it had a chance to get started. Then, in 1934, the government stepped in. Congress passed a law prohibiting airmail contractors from being associated with aviation manufacturing companies. The fledgling conglomerate was split apart, leaving the Boeing Company as the blue-collar remnant of a dream, perched on what suddenly seemed to be the edge of the world. William Boeing could still build planes, but he had no control over what happened to them. He had to be a salesman. Faced with this, the would-be empire builder simply quit; he resigned as chairman of the board and left the company faced with massive layoffs and holding only $582,000 in cash.

Claire Egtvedt was the president of the Boeing Company when William Boeing resigned. Egtvedt had been with Boeing from the war years; as a young University of Washington graduate he had been hired as chief engineer. He had weathered the postwar slump of 1919, when the company was almost literally reduced to making furniture, Bill Boeing was paying salaries out of his personal checking account, and the engineering department was down to two employees. In fact, according to Harold Mansfield in his book *Vision*, at the depth of that 1919 crisis Egtvedt made an interesting—particularly interesting when looked at from the vantage point of the experience of Boeing engineers of the 1960s and seventies—and impassioned plea to William Boeing:

> We are building airplanes, not cement sidewalks. If you want to build cement sidewalks and just do work requiring a minimum of engineering, then you can do away with engineering. Do away with it. Just mix the materials, pour them into a form and collect your money. But if you want to build and sell airplanes, you first have

to create them. That takes research and development and testing and engineering. The airplane isn't half what it ought to be. Can't we hire a few engineers and try to build a future?

Feeling that way, it was no wonder that when he was faced with the responsibility for saving a crippled company in 1934 Egtvedt's eyes and heart should turn to a familiar source for inspiration. To quote Mansfield again:

> He looked out of his window across Engineering to the shops, thinking of the men there and the planes they had built. There was no notion of defeat in them. Some of them came in and suggested a plan of alternating work, one group on for two weeks, then off, while the other group worked the next two—to preserve the staff. When the plan was put into effect, many of them came down on their time off and worked without pay.

Without a mention of union action.

If William Boeing could blame the government for ruining his dream monopoly, Claire Egtvedt would thank the government and, later, World War II for bringing the Boeing Company to the point where in 1945 the payroll was over half a million dollars a day. At which point the war ended and the government stopped ordering warplanes. The guaranteed sales boom ended for the company and it was confronted by another crisis. It also had a new president—William Allen.

Allen had been the company lawyer since the time of Bill Boeing and, reluctance to take the job and disclaimers aside, when he accepted the presidency on September 5, 1945, there was no doubt that he was a complete company man. He had even made a list of the things he should do if the job were offered:

Must keep temper—always—never get mad.

Be considerate of my associates' views.

Don't talk too much—let others talk.

Don't be afraid to admit that you don't know.

Don't get immersed in detail—concentrate on the big objectives.

Make contacts with other people in industry—and keep them!

Make a sincere effort to understand labor's viewpoint.

Be definite; don't vacillate.

Act—get things done—move forward.

Develop a postwar future for Boeing.

Try hard, but don't let obstacles get you down. Take things in stride.

Above all else be human—keep your sense of humor—learn to relax.

Be just; straightforward; invite criticism and learn to take it.

Be confident. Having once made the move, make the most of it.

Bring to task great enthusiasm, unlimited energy.

Make Boeing even greater than it is. . . .

In Allen, Boeing had a president who knew the business, respected the professionals and, most of all, was not too proud to be a salesman.

By 1945, not quite a hundred years after its first settlers, Seattle had found its place in the American economy and, in that place, its claim to permanence as an American city. There was no longer any danger of the city being merely an outpost on the edge of the civilized continent. It was central to America because it had a product. And not a product that could be exhausted (like lumber or minerals), or a product that would flame, burn, and die with passing fashions. Seattle's product—the means of transportation, vehicles to move things and people—was limited only by the saleability of the results of practical human imagination.

The growth and realization of Seattle's economic bases through its first hundred years seem so natural that they almost appear to have been planned from the landing of the Denny party. All the elements of the structure of the Boeing Company can be imagined springing—like Athena from the brow of Zeus—fully realized from the fertile mind of Arthur Denny.

Arthur Denny wanted to build a city and he wanted intelligent, hard-working companions to help him. The emphasis in his mind was really on the compatibility of prospective fellow-citizens—Denny wanted people in Seattle whom he could live with as well as work with. As he put it, in *Pioneer Days on Puget Sound* (1888):

> The man who had the best stock of health and the most faith and pluck, was the most wealthy, for we were all capitalists in those days. Each one expected to help himself, and as a rule all went to work with energy to open up the country and make homes for themselves, and at the same time they were ever ready to help each other in case of need or misfortune, and I will presume to say that if the people now possessed more of the spirit that then actuated the "old moss backs," as some reproachfully style the old settlers, we would hear less about a conflict between labor and capital, which in truth is largely a conflict between labor and laziness. We had no eight hour, nor even ten hour days then, and I never heard of anyone striking, not even an Indian except that every man who was worthy of the name (and I am proud to say

that there were few exceptions then,) was found striking squarely and determinedly at whatever obstacle stood in the way of his success.

It was a matter of like minds in like bodies working toward a common goal. In the infancy of Seattle, as Denny points out, there seemed to be an easy, natural harmony— a communality of purpose. As the city grew larger, its leaders tried to maintain the idea of unity—the Seattle Spirit. But the gap between word and deed grew greater with each civic boom and bust. Seattle got everything it wanted: recognition, access to the rest of the nation, and viable products for the base of its economy. And it was situated in a startlingly beautiful and livable geographic location. It would have been ideal for a small community of very intelligent and very rich men served by robots.

Seattle traditionally recruited residents; from Henry Yesler, through the seduction of coastal shipyard workers, to the nationwide ad campaign for young engineers in the 1950s and sixties, the city searched for the right type of resident—one who would fit in. That there turned out to be too many young, clean, ambitious, well-educated, and right-thinking citizens for any city to handle can hardly be blamed on growing, hustling Seattle. The city tried very hard to lure only the very best, and it got them.

The Boeing Company and the city of Seattle rode several simultaneously cresting waves in the fifties and sixties. The Russian fever/Sputnik scare phase of the Cold War brought about a great fear of a technological gap between the United States and the Soviet Union and filled American engineering schools to overflowing. Boeing took the cream from the top, turning hordes of young (and some not-so-young) engineers and technicians loose on projects ranging from space missiles to futuristic passenger planes.

The beauty of the Sound area, coupled with a good job,

made Boeing and Seattle seem irresistible, and people
flocked to the city. Then, in terrifying succession, the airlines stopped buying planes, the government cut back on
the space program, and, finally, Congress vetoed (for eco-
logic and economic reasons) the biggest airplane of all—the
Boeing Supersonic Transport. Boeing responded with
massive employee layoffs.

The extent of these layoffs may be seen in a release of
Boeing Company job force figures from 1966 to mid-1972
(these figures are only for the Boeing Company in the State
of Washington; they do not reflect the layoffs of satellite
corporations or marginally dependent industries or businesses).

Year	Hired/ Rebired	Attrition Laid Off	Total	Net Change	Ending Population
1966	54,000	1,300	29,200	+24,800	88,400
1967	37,000	500	24,500	+12,500	100,900
1968	21,600	1,800	27,000	−5,400	95,500
1969	7,700	5,400	22,800	−15,100	80,400
1970	1,600	28,400	35,700	−34,100	46,300
1971	3,800	9,500	12,000	−8,200	38,100
1972 (1st 5 mo.)	2,700	350	1,400	+1,300	39,400

Peter Bush, director of public relations for the Boeing
Company, described the meaning and effect of attrition/
layoffs:

> ... layoffs didn't begin until the Seattle area pay-
> roll got down to the neighborhood of 80,000. The
> turnover was so great at the 100,000 peak that just
> turning down the hiring spigot got us down to the
> 80,000 figure without causing any hardship to any-
> one on the payroll. The 80,000 down to 60,000 cut-
> back still had a lot of attrition in it but began some

real hurt in the community because the spending level began to tail off and marginal businesses such as car dealerships who counted on Boeing employing three members of a family instead of two or one had to cut back sharply too.

But, in retrospect, it was the 60,000 down to our low point where the real hardship commenced.

Families that had become accustomed to two cars suddenly had none, the bountiful suburbs became jungles of for sale signs, and people used to going to the Space Needle for Sunday brunch were locking their doors and pulling down their blinds. Those who were let go were the type of residents Arthur Denny had dreamed of for his city of the future, the type Claire Egtvedt wanted to hire, the type Thomas Burke would have invited to a dinner honoring Jim Hill—they were, in the main, white-collar workers, "good people" or "good people's neighbors." They could see the good life that had been theirs going on around them, mocking them. They felt ashamed, personally more than professionally, and carried their hurt like a blot on their lives.

Bill Brammer, a former technical writer for Boeing, described what happened:

B.B.: This thing happened around 1968 through 1970, when the company was really in bad shape. We lost a number of contracts and everybody knew that sooner or later you were going to go. Then you just sort of sat around and waited for that hand on the shoulder to tell you that this was your last day.

Q.: They're not supposed to give you two weeks' notice?

B.B.: Well, yes, they try to. In fact, they give you more than that. Sometimes it's a month ahead. And one of the things that they did do, in spite of all the bad things that happened, they did call in representatives from other businesses all over the place and had them gather in this gigantic Plant 2 cafeteria and set up booths so that they could interview people on the way out and try to get these people lined up in other jobs. The hell of it was that there were no other jobs in aerospace and 90 percent of these guys were aerospace types and all they did was take résumés and take them back to their particular companies and file them. That's exactly what happened. A lot of these guys never heard from these companies. The way I feel personally, I was loyal to the company because I liked it. I liked what they were doing. But I had qualms about working in aerospace because I didn't like to have to do with the missile thing. The airplane division was fine. But one is destructive and the other is productive and I didn't particularly like this. I had been in the war, World War Two, and I had my fill of destructive hardware. My family was terribly upset by this thing and we were thrown into a state of practically no money coming in. We didn't get on welfare but we did get our food stamps.

I was drawing unemployment compensation and after all of our resources were exhausted, including borrowing on my G.I. insurance until it was practically defunct, we borrowed money from neighbors and friends. Just trying to stay alive. Right in the middle of the unemployment thing, I got this telegram from the company. I had borrowed some money to put a roof on my house from the credit union and they decided that we were kind of juggling a little bit, and whenever a payment would become delinquent, I would be reminded of it by a letter. So I missed two payments in a row and I got this telegram saying: call this number immediately. And this guy says, you owe us this money. Let's get it here and now or we are going to have to take legal action. And this is after working for a company for fifteen years.

The hell of it is the company always overhired. At the beginning of the 707 program, they hired something like seven hundred industrial engineers. And after about the first four or five airplanes were coming down the assembly line, and the bugs were primarily out of the thing, they dumped about three or four hundred of them. These guys were from Michigan, all over, hell, some foreigners. And this happens a lot of times. They are here a couple of years and that's the end of them. But Boeing will never tell them this, of course. So, really, I think some of these guys are hired under false pretenses. Of course, they get moving expenses but . . .

Chuck Eberhardt, an ex-Boeing employee, the head of the North Shore Multi-Service Agency in 1972, talked of the psychological effect—of what the laid-off employee would and should do:

Call me a research analyst, assistant analyst perhaps. Moving around through Boeing, one does acquire half a dozen titles doing the same thing. And when one also acquires the title of "unemployed" there arises a pure, unadulterated fear that one will blackball himself in naming names or in appearing on an investigative committee, or in trying to watchdog Boeing in some way to correct abuses or uncover them.

First of all, in the American system of employment, you bear in mind that an employment record is the single dominating thing in a person's life. So from the standpoint of fear and not being able to get a job, fear of laying it on the line, yes, it is there and there is no doubt about it. The opportunities for re-employment—whatever they may be, generally speaking—are so limited here, in my own viewpoint, they might as well just face up to it that they are cooked. They're done, they're dead until they get out of this idea that they are going to get back to Boeing.

They are not going to make it. Boeing is going out right now to hire some new people. I think it said in the Seattle First National Bank forecast here for the month, I believe Boeing says that they are going to hire something in the order of five thousand people and they will have to go outside the local area to do it. In other words, Boeing is going out nationally and advertising that it is hiring again.

Boeing is looking out for itself, first, last, and always. It has to be accountable to its stockholders; any employer is. If an employer doesn't have the right essentially to hire who he wants to hire, he is no longer himself. But these individuals who have reached the magical age of forty-five, who have been dumped, there is no economic reason in the world for Boeing ever to hire them back, never really. And for them to hang on with that thread that I was the best program planner, or that I was the best budget man, that I was the best systems engineer, and I'm going to get hired back when the umpteenth airplane contract comes along, it's a fading dream.

I know. I was with Employment Security for three months downtown and there is no way to break that dream that they have. The only way that

that is ever going to happen is for them to go through the complete process of degeneration down to the point I've done: I'm cooked, I've had it, I might as well go out and convert myself into something that is usable. Something that is usable generally speaking is not how do you stretch this wire from this point to that sheet of metal over there and make it move à la engineering.

But there is a variety of alternative things to be done. The job clinic here—we can't find jobs here for engineers. There are no engineering jobs open. The ones that are open, Boeing systems has already taken care of. So they have to face up. Either they are going to go fishing or they are going to go logging or they are going to go out and really learn about life by starting all over again as a volunteer someplace. And build their own thing out of it. Whatever it may be. And I think I see so much in need in the whole complex of government and of the services that are required, that people can learn about. Admittedly, it is a school of hard knowledge, a volunteering program. But it's a way to find out what they want to do and go at it and do it until they have learned enough that they can offer somebody their services and get a buck for it. And it's no easy thing. But to hang on to the dream that sooner or later another project is going to come along, they are wasting and wasting away.

In reality they probably have more talent within them than they ever realized if they would just step away from that damn Talent-Plus and even go down to maybe the Port of Seattle, or go down to the airport, or go down to a fishing fleet and say I want to volunteer: I will come down here eight hours a day for the next six months. I really want to learn about this thing. And a whole new Pandora's box comes open.

But they won't listen to these kinds of words. And the only way it is going to happen is when they have drained their last resource and then they are really an object of pity. And then they finally will say, "My God, what can I do?" and you have to say to them, "Well, you can do this. You can sit here and shuffle papers, learning how to put together an old dossier." I still have friends among the laid-off and I say, "Do you want a job?" And they say, "Yes, I want a job." And I say, "Well, come on in and sit down and work for a while."

While ex-employees like Brammer and Eberhardt talked about Boeing, the company was busy diversifying. In the spring of 1973, young Seattle lawyer-realtor Warren Holtz felt almost optimistic about it:

As far as Boeing's diversification goes, probably the first step out of pure airplane manufacturing for Boeing was the development of several different types of hydrofoils. Then they went into the container business and here last month, believe it or not, they went into the real estate business. They have been buying up big chunks of land on the east side of Lake Washington. They are not only going to landscape it but they are going to put up houses. The only thing that they are not going to do, the government won't let them, they're not going to sell them. They've contracted out with the realtors to sell them. But this is going to be one of their real big diversifications.

The government won't let Boeing or any large company step in and monopolize any segment of the economy. They will let them build but not take over a complete building and selling operation.

They are working now on an air car. What they have done really is take all of that surplus money and they are beating it into other channels. There is still one big building force in our economy, that's true, but it's got a lot of fingers now. And you can chop off one without impairing the effectiveness of the others, I think.

Henry Broderick, wealthy pioneer realtor and investor, took a view seasoned by time and a thorough understanding of economics:

H.B.: People are always talking about Boeing diversifying. Why, they don't seem to know that back twenty years ago Boeing had that idea in mind. I remember when they opened their Science Building down there and Bill Allen and I were walking along the hallway and there were a lot of cubicles with one desk and one chair only. I said, "Bill, what's that fellow doing in there now?" And he said, "I wish you hadn't asked me that. I don't know what the hell he is doing." He said, "You know something, we have about twenty-five or thirty of these fellows in these little cubicles and we tell them to get in there, they are scientists, they're being paid to think. We don't care what they want to think about. We don't want them to think planes. Think of something else. Anything else. We don't care what."

Q.: A think tank.

H.B.: Yes. He said, "There are a lot of them. I don't know what they are thinking about." You see, Boeing had that in mind a long time ago. A lot of people think that they are very smart by saying that they think Boeing should diversify. Well, the Boeings are no fools. They are not going to diversify just to suit the city of Seattle and perhaps lose a lot of money. They are not going to go to anything if there is not going to be some profit in it.

Nobody expects, or even wants, a city or a corporation to act the understanding, doting father. But there is an absolute coldness, a frighteningly methodical dehumanization about the way the city of Seattle achieved its goals that makes even "survival of the fittest" seem charitable in contrast. The people Boeing (or Yesler, or the shipyards) fired were, after all, *asked* to come to Seattle—recruited away from other lives—to be more than employees; to be, in feeling if not in fact, members of a family, not a corporation. Yet when Thomas Burke talks about the city, or when Henry Broderick talks about the Boeing Company, they are talking about thinking, acting entities—the Boeing Company *is* alive and so much more important than its individual human components that, as Holtz says, "you can chop off one without impairing the effectiveness of the others."

Ex-newspaperman Terry Pettus has spent most of his life walking in the shadow of the company:

It seems to me that you won't find too many big cities in the United States that are company cities. We weren't a company town. A company town is one thing; a company city is quite another thing. I have been around company towns and God knows in the Northwest we have had our share of the lumber company towns, but Boeing was dominating a city. . . . For example, Boeing had a policy for its executive and white-collar workers—and re-

member, Boeing had more white-collar workers
than blue-collar workers. It was a classic example of
modern airplane technology. They used to boast
that Boeing had more Ph.D.'s than the University
of Washington and I'm sure it was true. They hired
brains and technical ability, so consequently they
had an enormous reservoir of emissaries to domi-
nate a community by virtue of participating in local
affairs. You know they even had a political action
committee going under the guise of nonpartisan-
ship. They would give these executives and middle
executives and starting-to-be-executives and their
white-collar people time to go to these classes on
political action. Well, they did it apparently up until the big boom and maybe they still do it. They
were very careful not to tell you who to vote for or
what party to work in, but just carry the old business spirit into your community—into the political
parties. For example, in every community, when
you want to, when you have got the manpower and
the womanpower to distribute that weight, you can
have an enormous influence and Boeing operated in
the same way that newspapers operated—you know
that if you have been a newspaper person. I worked
for seven daily newspapers. I never had any editor
tell me what the policy of the paper was. You know
they think that if you are too damn dumb to figure
that out you are too damn dumb to be working
there. So Boeing operated the same way.

Here is an example of a friend of mine. The family very tragically had a spastic child and they lived
in the Queen Anne neighborhood over here, upper-
middle-class, middle-class neighborhood, and they
found out that there were a number of families with
that problem and there was a Seattle or King

County Spastic Society. Well, this woman got interested in it and she was something of a left-winger. She eventually ended up on the executive committee of one of the spastic organizations—seven people, five of them Boeing. She came to tell me that story and I said, well, I can believe it. You go anywhere where there is any type of activity going on and by the very weight of these people, Boeing controls Seattle.

Oh God, and it is a blighting effect.

Paths to the Breadline

People used to claim—Arthur Denny's voice loudest among them—that in Seattle's infancy there were no problems between labor and management because everybody worked. Maybe it was true, but those fourteen- to sixteen-hour days turned a tidy profit for some and not too much for others. It probably seemed all right when the boss was working right alongside you, but it became a very different matter when he decided to sit down and watch, or head uptown to tend to other business interests. Paranoia, although they didn't know the word, set in, and people began to realize that they were "workers" who had "bosses," and that it wasn't just one big happy family. Naturally, those who had reached the promised land first had a much better idea of what they were doing than those who followed. Plus —and it was a big plus—they had the land: taken by fiat, or Divine Right, or whatever you want to call it. It was theirs.

They knew it right away, but it took those who were working, not with them as they first thought but for them, a bit longer to catch on. Once the workers found out, labor problems erupted.

It has always been an American problem that those who have don't want to give it up, and those who don't have want it. Nobody in the land of the free really wants to work for anybody else, particularly when that anybody else isn't giving any evidence of working. Seattle may have been a little rougher than some of its eastern cousins but it was, after all, the last port of call in America, and nobody really wanted to go back to Chicago, not to mention New York or any of the other cities they had left behind. So people stayed, and when they realized what was going on, they stayed to fight.

The General Strike of 1919. There were problems before and, God knows, problems after, but Seattle's labor history will probably be best remembered for the General Strike, America's first. It wasn't because of the violence of the strike, because there really was none, nor was it due to hardships inflicted, because the strikers went out of their way to insure that the city would not be destroyed, but because of the way it happened.

In 1893, James Hill brought his railroad to its western terminus in Seattle, thereby eliminating Tacoma, Portland, Bellingham, and all the rest of Seattle's rivals from the competition. Seattle had become the link to the rich East Coast. In 1897, the Klondike gold rush hit and Seattle was in business in a way it had never dreamed of. As a direct result of these two happenings, Seattle's population jumped from 42,000 in 1890 to 237,194 in 1910. A staggering growth. To some of the dreamy old-timers it meant that theirs was now truly a city. But to many of the hard-thinking newcomers, the rapid growth raised more problems than it solved.

First of all, Seattle was not an industrial city. Overnight it found itself transformed from a frontier logging post into a massive hick town. The town had existed for years to serve the needs of San Francisco. Suddenly, it was on its own, and all it had to offer was timber and good will.

Not enough. The city grew so fast that its socks didn't fit anymore. Seattle, probably more than any other American city, needed a war. And got it. And with it, jobs on the docks building ships for the government. For a while that more than sufficed, but when the Great War ended, the workers realized that the Great Father in Washington no longer needed them.

There was a massive labor force in Seattle at the end of World War I and it was being taught a lesson that would be repeated time and time again. There were no jobs. But there were unions: the powerful AFL, holding a firm hand over the docks; and the IWW, come "down from the woods"; and there were newspapers and individuals willing to risk their own flesh in defiance. And there was Russia.

The overthrow of the Czarist tradition and the disaster of Kerensky certainly did more good for Seattle labor than harm. When the U.S.A. stuck its pristine hands into the mud of the Russian revolution, it brought about the brotherhood of labor that the afflicted, out-of-work laborers in Seattle had dreamed of. The IWW (Wobblies) could hold brotherly hands with the AFL, while the federal government, which had bestowed its bounties upon Seattle during the war years, suddenly withdrew its paternal hand. And Seattle turned Red. AFL members, already angered by the forced patriotism of the war years, were ready to be radicalized, and the Wobblies were there.

It was an uneasy alliance. The AFL wanted complete

control. The IWW and the independent radicals didn't want to give it to them. But there had to be a way to show the city and the nation that they were all serious. The result was the General Strike.

How many actual "Communists" were involved remains to this day a moot point. What is important is that labor committed itself to a humane shutdown of a large city. After being beaten and kicked and herded like sheep, they showed they wanted humanity.

It all began with the shipyards. Throughout its history, Seattle has always seemed to belong to one industry or another. Even in its nonindustrial infancy, the town had its timber, and later it became a safe harbor for those dazed by the gold rush. But the shipyards during World War I changed the nature of the city forever. Seattle had been gradually building a domestic labor force, but it was not prepared for the enormous demands of government contracts for shipbuilding, either in the number of ships required or in the speed of delivering them. This meant Seattle had to recruit outsiders. The recruitment was successful, and Seattle took great pride that it contributed 26.5 percent of all the ships produced for the Emergency Fleet Corporation, and that it could send out metal freighters in seventy-eight days.

But the boom brought about problems between the older, established citizens and the new arrivals. The newcomers were recruited, "skilled men," not like the Chinese who came with the railroad and worked cheaper than anyone else and who could, if necessary, be herded on to ships and sent back to China. The imported shipworkers and allied tradesmen wanted to stay in Seattle and, on the whole, they were "native-born Americans," but the older residents could not in the boom years personally screen the vast numbers who came. Would these workers be desirable residents of the new Queen City of the West?

There were monumental housing problems; old-line merchants raised prices for new faces; Seattleites started looking suspiciously at their neighbors. And the business-men started looking with horror and fear at the unions.

One thing that Arthur Denny and his contemporaries hoped to avoid was a city of laborers who did not want to labor. This spirit passed down from the first generation to the second. There was to be no conflict between labor and management. And conflict was precisely, at least as the older generation saw it, what the unions wanted. It was frightening for both sides.

Union power was concentrated in the shipyards, and it was there also that the greatest number of "imports" worked, most of them having left places like San Francisco and Portland on the promise of higher wages. As tensions grew between the old-timers and the newcomers, everyone seemed to be waiting for the war to end, and not necessarily for patriotic reasons.

Some of the old-time residents declared that shipbuild-ing didn't belong in the core of the city they envisioned, and that once the undesirable transients left Seattle could again choose who its citizens might be. Others felt that shipbuilding was the industry the city had been looking for since its birth and that giving it up would ring a death knell to progress.

Local labor had its own fight with the Emergency Fleet Corporation, the government-controlled shipbuilding au-thority. And even within the local unions themselves there was strife.

But on January 21, 1919, the Metal Trades Council went on strike, and 35,000 people were no longer working in Seattle. No ships were being built.

The General Strike brought into the limelight two very strong and conflicting personalities—Ole Hanson and Anna Louise Strong.

If personal and family background can serve as any kind of guide to a person's behavior and political actions, then Anna Louise Strong would seem to have been a very implausible, if not impossible, radical. Robert Friedheim describes her early life in *The Seattle General Strike:*

> Her family could be traced back to settlers arriving in New England in 1630. Her father was one of the most prominent clergymen in Seattle, known for his theological liberalism; her brother was a rising young man in the YMCA movement. After a year at Bryn Mawr, she graduated from Oberlin College. She was one of the earlier woman PhD's, taking her degree at the University of Chicago. Her early career reflected the family background—her dissertation was entitled "A Study of Prayer from the Standpoint of Social Psychology," her first job, associate editor of *Advance*, a Protestant fundamentalist weekly newspaper. Later she was active in child-welfare work, setting up exhibits organized by the United States Child Welfare Bureau.
>
> In 1915, when her father was called to a Seattle congregation, Anna Louise accompanied him. She immediately threw herself into organizations devoted to civic improvement. She organized "Know Your City" trips to acquaint Seattleites with the beauties and facilities of the Queen City. Because of her humanitarian work with civic and child-welfare organizations and the fact that she was one of the best educated women in town, she was elected to the Seattle school board with the solid backing of women's, civic and good-government organizations.

Yet those very qualities—her humanitarianism and her intelligence—that made her the darling of safe, progressive liberalism in Seattle, made her, in the reactionary aftermath of the General Strike, anathema. She began by drifting to the left and ended in persecution and self-imposed exile, first in Russia and then China. She was ostracized because of her conviction that the system she had been working in was at fault, and because of what she wrote in an editorial for the Seattle paper, the *Union Record,* which appeared on February 4, 1919:

There will be many cheering and there will be some who fear.

Both of these emotions are useful, but not too much of either.

We are undertaking the most tremendous move ever made by LABOR in this country, a move which will lead —NO ONE KNOWS WHERE!

We do not need hysteria.

We need the iron march of labor.

LABOR WILL FEED THE PEOPLE.

Twelve great kitchens have been offered, and from them food will be distributed by the provisions trades at low cost to all.

LABOR WILL CARE FOR THE BABIES AND THE SICK.

The milk-wagons and the laundry drivers are arranging plans for supplying milk to babies, invalids and hospitals, and taking care of the cleaning of linen for hospitals.

LABOR WILL PRESERVE ORDER.

The strike committee is arranging for guards, and it is expected that the stopping of the cars will keep people at home.

A few hot-headed enthusiasts have complained that strikers only should be fed, and the general public left to endure severe discomfort. Aside from the inhumanitarian character of such suggestions, let us get this straight—

NOT THE WITHDRAWAL OF LABOR POWER, BUT THE POWER OF THE STRIKERS TO MANAGE WILL WIN THIS STRIKE.

What does Mr. Piez of the Shipping Board care about the closing down of Seattle's shipyards, or even of all the industries of the northwest? Will it not merely strengthen the yards at Hog Island, in which he is more interested?

When the shipyard owners of Seattle were on the point of agreeing with the workers, it was Mr. Piez who wired them that, if they so agreed—

HE WOULD NOT LET THEM HAVE STEEL.

Whether this is camouflage we have no means of knowing. But we do know that the great eastern combinations of capitalists COULD AFFORD to offer privately to Mr. Skinner, Mr. Ames and Mr. Duthrie a few millions apiece in the eastern shipyard stock.

RATHER THAN LET THE WORKERS WIN.

The closing down of Seattle's industries, as a MERE SHUTDOWN, will not affect these eastern gentlemen much. They could let the whole northwest go to pieces, as far as money alone is concerned.

BUT, the closing down of the capitalistically controlled industries of Seattle, while the WORKERS ORGANIZE to feed the people, to care for the babies and the sick, to preserve order—THIS will move them, for this looks too much like the taking over of POWER by the workers.

Labor will not only SHUT DOWN the industries, but Labor will REOPEN, under the management of the appropriate trades, such activities as are needed to preserve public health and public peace. If the strike continues, Labor may feel led to avoid public suffering by reopening more and more activities.

UNDER ITS OWN MANAGEMENT.

And that is why we say that we are starting on a road that leads—NO ONE KNOWS WHERE!

That "NO ONE KNOWS WHERE!" scared the pants off Seattle. They then saw that revolution was at hand, and no matter what labor said, the city fathers knew full well that their city and their money were in grave danger. A shutdown would bring disaster to the fine houses on the hills. All of a sudden they were living in Russia, not in their rich, semivirgin wilderness, where they could control everything that happened. "Foreigners" were nipping at their flanks, and a giant Red overcoat seemed to have been spread over the city. It was the first major Communist scare in America, and Seattle, particularly Mayor Ole Hanson, made the most of it. It was one more chance to put Seattle firmly on the map.

The Seattle *Post-Intelligencer* reprinted "NO ONE KNOWS WHERE!" the next day, and Seattleites prepared themselves for the revolution. They emptied store shelves of food, bought guns in massive numbers, and the rich simply decided to leave town for the duration.

On February 6, 1919, it happened. The city was shut down. But the strike was short-lived; at noon February 11, all except the shipyard workers returned to work. Even in locking up the city, the same 65,000 workers who had walked off their jobs had kept the city alive. There had been no real need for the guns behind closed shutters, or the quick and expensive trips to Portland. The wealthy had been safe all along. Of course, the shipyard workers were left to wither, as the federal government—no longer trusting a city that could allow itself, even for a few days, to be taken over by Bolsheviks—pulled out the plug and forgot about Seattle as a shipbuilding center. The out-of-work could no longer strike, because there were no jobs—all they could do was leave.

To quote Robert L. Friedheim from *The Seattle General Strike:*

> No single element caused the Seattle general strike. It occurred only because there was a multiplicity of causes —IWW propaganda which gave Northwest workers name familiarity with the general strike; the class spirit and advanced opinions of Seattle workers; the emotional

impact of the Bolshevik Revolution; general world un-
rest; and obdurate positions taken by the shipyard owners; the intervention of Charles Piez and the United
States government; fear of employer support for a growing open-shop movement; agitation by revolutionary and
nonrevolutionary radicals among local labor; and the distinctive Seattle AFL organization, led by James A. Duncan and his progressives, which insisted that all Seattle
workers pull together and which provided a vehicle for
such unity. Separately, not even the dominant causes
would have provoked the general strike; rather, it was
the combination of extraordinary events and the condition of Seattle labor.

Why the General Strike had to happen is a subject of
debate to this day. Ostensibly it began with the walkout of
the shipyard workers, who were angered by the refusal of
the government to grant them a higher wage scale than
their East Coast brethren. But that apparently simple action seems clouded over with differences of interpretation.
Seattle, largely due to the efforts of James Duncan and his
moderate independence from the doctrine of the parent
AFL, had been a very unified town for some years. Duncan
and the "Duncanites" on the Seattle Central Labor Council
saw to it that labor took a united and progressive stance.
But Duncan and Harry Ault, editor of the *Union Record*, the
only labor-owned daily in the country, were away in Chicago attending a conference protesting the imprisonment
of Tom Mooney, the San Francisco AFL leader accused of
murder. With them were twenty-three others. So the Central Labor Council was in effect leaderless and wide open
for radical takeover when the crisis erupted. Some older
labor leaders argued against the strike, saying that since the
war was over they would be fighting for wage increases in
jobs that would no longer exist.

But it was too late. The strike hit, and before Duncan

was able to stop it the damage had been done. Some blame the strike on Leon Green, the shadowy Communist who appeared in Seattle about three months before the strike and disappeared shortly after. But, as Friedheim has pointed out, there were too many disparate elements leading up to the strike to pinpoint one person as the sole cause, whether that person was Anna Louise Strong or Leon Green. Both of them were extremely useful, however, to Mayor Ole Hanson and the incipient reactionism of Seattle.

With names like Green and Strong, it was easy to evoke the fear of the Red Menace. And even after Green had disappeared and Strong had been acquitted of sedition charges, the reactionaries could still scream that the labor movement was filled with Communists, and that it must clean house or have the cleaning done for it. The strike ended, but the conflict had just begun. As Ole Hanson said, "Labor must clean house. Seattle may forgive, but it cannot forget." While Ole raced around the country preaching the fear of Communism to native-born Americans, Seattle went about the business of witch-hunting on a major scale and the once solid "Duncanite" AFL leaders found themselves splitting into factions, each demanding different things. When the Central Labor Council controlled the town, it was able to hold the radical and conservative elements together under one progressive banner, but after the General Strike everyone was running scared. The Council's conservative faction knew that the Red smear of the strike persisted in the city's mind, so they truly did have to purge themselves of any connection with the radicals. That left the Central Labor Council in the exact position the establishment wanted it: lame duck.

The shutdown of the shipyards didn't help at all. It was expected that with the war's end government ship orders would disappear, but in a canny move the government managed to shift the blame to the strike. The Emergency Fleet Corporation did, in fact, make good its warnings to stop construction of boats being built in Seattle yards because of the strike, but of course the corporation had planned on doing it anyway. Skinner and Eddy, the largest of the shipyards, was put out of business by government foreclosure.

In 1919, Seattle had more than 40,000 industrial workers; by 1921 that number had dwindled to barely more than 13,000. The reason in most people's minds—the strike. People simply could not accept the wartime boom as no more than that, leaving in its wake dead industries. The city felt it was being punished for putting a scar on the nation. It had made a mistake. It would make no more.

Labor had no bargaining power, particularly with the government as management; nonlabor hated it for destroying the city. It seemed, for a time, that everything was over. With people snarling about revolution and laughing at the unions' impotence, labor had to sit back and think, to find some way of regaining all it had lost in the strike. The answer that came was politics.

For a while it was a disaster. As Bert Swain has said, "It was fully twenty years before labor recovered from the unfortunate effects of the strike." But there was something formed called the Triple Alliance—the state AFL, the railroad workers, and the state Grange. And following that, the Washington Commonwealth Federation, whose aim was to influence selection of local and state candidates and their platforms.

It took fires, gold rushes, wars, and blatant racism to open the schism between employee and employer. But once opened it remained. No one has calculated how many hours of work it took the Triple Alliance and the Commonwealth Federation to try to convince farmers, loggers, dock workers, indeed all the labor force of the State of Washington, that they had a common cause—unjust treatment at the hands of management, whether it be the individual boss or local or federal government; to show the workers that their problem was not one, as Arthur Denny had seen it, between "labor and laziness," but clearly a battle between the employer and the employee—between the exploiter who constantly denied that he was doing anything of the sort and the exploited whose very lives affirmed that exploitation was precisely what was happening.

All the Commonwealth Federation's efforts failed and eventually it voted to dissolve itself, but its demise was not as important as its existence for a number of years. James Farley may or may not have called the State of Washington "The Soviet of Washington" in apposition to the other forty-seven states, but someone did and it was, in many ways, a just and apt comment. The "Soviet" failed because it finally ran scared and bowed down to Big Brother in the form of the pre-McCarthy Canwell Committee (Canwell was a petty, ambitious man from Spokane, a man not unlike Ole Hanson) and in a more grotesque way to HUAC and the genuine terror of McCarthyism. People were literally taken from their houses at night, not by men in jackboots, but by men in business suits, showing cards. And asked to testify.

The son of a midwestern minister, Terry Pettus came to Seattle with his wife Berta in 1927, and began an illustrious (if checkered) career in the Northwest as a radical newspaperman, working first for the Seattle *Star,* next for the Tacoma *Daily & Sunday Ledger,* and then he and his wife ran the *Willapa Harbor Pilot* in South Bend. He was one of the original organizers of the Newspaper Guild in Seattle and along the coast and served as its provisional president, steering the Guild through the famous strike against the Hearst-owned Seattle *Post-Intelligencer* in 1936, for which he was permanently blackballed in the daily newspaper field.

He was also editor of the Washington Commonwealth Federation's weekly paper, the *New Dealer*. In 1953 he was convicted under the Smith Act as one of the Seattle Seven of "conspiring to teach and advocate the overthrow" of the United States government and sentenced to five years in prison (plus three more for contempt of court). On appeal, the verdict and the case were nullified.

He now lives in a houseboat, filled with his collection of early Kenneth Callahan paintings, on Lake Union (an "active working lake") in the center of the city where he is head of the Floating Homes Association. Mr. Pettus, who looks like a taller, thinner version of Ernest Hemingway, is part pragmatist, part idealist, a firm believer in America's precinct politics where "the informed amateur" can employ the art of the possible for the direct and visible benefit of the immediate community. This is how he recalls his case and the curious circumstances that surrounded it.

T.P.: I joined the Communist Party in 1938 down in South Bend and I resigned twenty years later. My criticism of the Party is directed mainly at the leadership hierarchy—I think they have a lot of sins to account for. But in '48, when they were starting to indict Party leaders all over the country, I didn't have the courage to resign: you don't run under fire. Whenever the heat would go down they'd fan the thing so they'd get another batch of indictments, and finally in '52 they got around to us. Jesus, the Party was so filled with FBI agents that at each trial all these good comrades turned out to be stool pigeons, and in my case the first witness against me was an *officer* of the Party, a black man named Clark Harper.

They arrested us on Bill of Rights Day—September 21. Carly Larson, president of the International

Woodworkers' district council, was arrested smack in the middle of a union convention in Portland. Bill Pennoff, president of the Pension Union, was arrested at his home in Seattle and they picked up Johnny Dashpaw, the state chairman of the Civil Rights Congress [the organization that replaced the ACLU when it decided not to defend Communism]. I was arrested in Minneapolis in the home of my brother-in-law, a very staunch Catholic business-man who loved me in spite of my politics. Four FBI agents crash in the bedroom door and the place is surrounded by cars—they need a maximum amount of that to attract publicity. They arrested Paul Boen, the only black arrested, who was working in Chicago, and a woman named Barbara Hartle, who had been a functionary of the Party, was arrested somewhere in Portland where she was working as a waitress, and a guy named Henry Huff. We were arrested under the Smith Act, which held that it is a felony to teach or advocate the violent overthrow of the United States government, but we *weren't* charged with actually teaching or advocating, we were charged with *conspiring* to teach and advocate —the conspiracy law.

Well, how do you prove intent? You prove it by overt acts, but my case also involved a State of Washington law that an editor is criminally and civilly responsible for everything that is in his pub-lication. So, as an "offer of proof," we got together the bound volumes of the *New Dealer*, the *New World*, and the daily *People's World* of which I was northwest editor and wheeled them into court on hand trucks—they must have been five feet high— to show that there was no place I had ever advocated or taught the overthrow of the government. But the judge just smiled and said, Mr. Pettus is not charged with that, he is charged with conspiring to do it sometime in the future!

This trial lasted from April to November—it was the longest criminal case in history; the prosecution read all kinds of esoteric documents and manifestos to the jury, including the proceedings of the Third International in Moscow in 1919—hell, these guys weren't even born then! Days would go by, reading Lenin and Macobovitch and some I never even heard of, stressing the words "revolution," "capitalist class," and so on, and those poor jurors sitting there shaking.

During the course of the trial, Bill Pennoff killed himself, which was a tragic thing—he was a beautiful, beautiful person. He had been scheduled to be the first to take the stand, and after his death I became the first to go up and actually try to defend myself. Testifying on your own behalf, you waive all your constitutional rights, but we thought we could explain to the jurors what we really believed. The first witness we called was a philosophy professor named Herbert J. Phillips, and he was to give "expert" testimony to counteract these distortions of Marxism as a body of thought, and when the prosecution got hold of him they said, were you ever a member of the Communist Party? The attorneys objected that this was improper questioning of an "expert witness" but Judge Lindberg overruled —he overruled us on everything. Phillips refused to answer and was sent to jail on criminal contempt of court. Next I took the stand and refused to answer the same question when they put it to me, so at the end of each day in court they would haul me into jail. Every day the judge would smile and say, now

Mr. Pettus and Mr. Phillips and (later) Mr. Dash-paw, you know you are carrying the keys to the jail in your own pocket, all you have to do is purge yourself of this contempt. And we'd go back to jail each night and tell the guys, hey, do you know we got the keys?

Finally, they brought us in for sentencing and gave us all the limit, five years, and a $10,000 fine, and in addition the judge sentenced Dashpaw and me to three years more for being in contempt of court, the sentences to run consecutively! Well, it was that of course that broke the ice. It took us quite a while to raise the money, $180,000, to get us all out of jail, and then the goddam appeal was very expensive too—I think it cost $14,000 just to buy the transcript! Then it took almost two years for the circuit court to act on our appeal and throw out the contempt charge, and it wasn't until a year later that the Supreme Court acted on the California Smith Act case, which was ahead of us, and threw it out too. Then the circuit court of appeals in San Francisco said we should never have been arrested, never have been indicted, never have been tried. And I said, how about us being reimbursed for all this has cost us? You admit now we were absolutely innocent people!

Unfortunately, during the time we were waiting for our appeals to be heard, poor Barbara Hartle caved in. Boom! One day we picked up the *P.-I.* about two weeks after we got her out on bail and there it is on the front page: Barbara tells all to the FBI, says that she and all the defendants are guilty. She rescinds her bail, goes into the court in front of that guy and tells him that she is guilty and wishes to withdraw her plea of not guilty. Well, she has

already got her five years. I don't know what the
FBI told her, they probably lied like hell, the poor
thing. She dropped out of the appeal and so what
did they do? They picked her up and flung her in
the goddam prison. They said we can get you out in
eighteen months, otherwise you will do the whole
goddam five years. They can get you on parole, you
know. So then she came out, but she served eighteen
months.

Q.: What did the rest of you do?

T.P.: We never did a thing and then she becomes the key
witness for the House Un-American Activities
Committee. They bring her right out to Seattle,
they put her on the witness stand, this House Un-
American Activities Committee, and she spills
names. The *Times* ran them all. They could run
pages of names. I don't see how, if she hadn't been
coached, she could remember so many names—it
was like a phone book. She had been a Party leader
for years and she mentioned people she'd recruited,
she gave names, names, names, and she even named
my sister, whose only crime had been to offer her
a job! That's when Eugene V. Dennett got named.

Barbara was a graduate of Pullman, the state university at Pullman. Went into the radical movement
during the Depression out of compassion and concern for people. When she joined the Communist
Party, for many years she was a functionary. She
was a paid functionary, there wasn't any doubt
about her, but that's why she had so many names to
give. God she gave names, told about how she recruited people, how they would resist joining the
Party and how she would persuade them. You destroy yourself. Think of what she lives with. She
did it to herself. But those are human weaknesses

and I'm not going to condemn them. My God, I'm not God.

Eugene V. Dennett, now retired from Bethlehem Steel, tells a different story of that same period. But in order to understand his decision to give testimony before the House Un-American Activities Committee, it is necessary to understand some of the particulars of his background:

E.V.D.: First let me go back to an experience I once had in school when I was a small child in Lynn, Massachusetts. During the First World War they circulated little cards to the children in school which said I am a one hundred percent American—the child was instructed to take that home and have his parents sign it and bring it back to school. Part of the reason for it was that strikes were breaking out in the mills that were around Fall River. When I took mine home, my father said, you can tell your teacher I am a Bolshevik. I went back and said that my father refused to sign because he is a Bolshevik and proud of it, and I was promptly expelled from the fifth grade and told by the truant officer that I would never be readmitted until my father signed that card. And my father said, well, what about your compulsory education law? It took two weeks of hassling before they finally ordered me back—my father never did sign it, but I got a taste of terror, of political intimidation. My father's attitude was that my family has always fought for this country, we have a proud tradition, we can trace our relatives back before the days of the Revolution. Our people came over here in 1630. We don't have to apologize to anyone; we can say, "This is an un-American thing *you* are asking *me* to do and I refuse to do it." . . . Because of that experience in school firsthand, and because my mother had to fight like hell to keep going at the factory until she was run over and killed, and because of the fact that when we moved West following the war in 1919 my father continued to subscribe to the socialist papers, the *Socialist Call* and the *Appeal to Reason* (both of which went out of business soon after the conclusion of World War One, but we still had the Butte *Daily Bulletin* and the *Producers' News* out of Plentywood, Montana), I kept reading them and learning all about the big fights that were going on: the attempts at intimidation and harassment of the workers, the Centralia Affair in which Wesley Everest was muti-lated and murdered by the Legionnaires.

. . . I was reading all about this business while we were suffering extreme poverty ourselves. We were here two years and we didn't even have a cow. In my growing years I didn't have milk when I needed it and I usually went to school with a headache because the food we were eating was just corn, beans, and potatoes. I was frequently invited to a neighbor's who would give me a square meal, and there were school lunches, but they were never quite adequate, so I went through all of my high school years trying to study while suffering from malnutrition—start to finish. . . . I never forgot what it is like to be living on the verge of disaster, and I took a lot of odd jobs while in school, which limits good scholarship, but I did the best I could and I came out all right. After I graduated from normal school, I taught for about four years just outside of Portland.

In about 1930, there was a mass arrest of so-called subversives in Portland, and because my father had been on the mailing lists for the *Daily Bulletin* and the *Producers' News*, he was contacted by the old International Labor Defense which was the legal defense arm of the Communists in the early days.

Anyhow, an appeal was sent to my father to come to the aid of these people who were being arrested and who were mainly aliens—Bulgarian, Hungarian. Their homelands were under fascist dictators at the time, and the Immigration Service proposed to deport them because they were Communists. If deported home, they would immediately be executed. So I went to that meeting instead of my father, and as I got acquainted with the members they invited me to join the Communist Party; the appeal at that time was that whenever the capitalistic oppressors tried to take some out of circulation, more masses joined. It is an idealistic concept, but it doesn't always work out.

But this Portland group did grow rather extensively as a consequence of this ongoing persecution. About three or four months after I joined the Party, they had a problem: Seattle was the northwest headquarters of the Party and the district organizer was a fellow by the name of Alex Norell, who was a very difficult man to get along with, and the person from Portland who he wanted to come up to Seattle to be director of agitprop didn't want the job. Because I had some education and a socialist background, a telegram arrived one day demanding that I come to Seattle as the agitprop director of the district. At first I didn't know what to make of it, but I thought, well, hell, I can't think of any possibility of ever doing a teaching job the way it really ought to be done, and I was only making a hundred and ten dollars a month—hardly enough to call a living.

To say the least, I was extremely politically naïve, and knew nothing about the fight between Stalin and Trotsky—nor the fact that if you didn't accept what was handed down, you were considered to be a violator. Very shortly after that, the person known as the organization director came around to me and said: You'll have to prove yourself. We need a section organizer in Bellingham. So I said, fine, and went up and stayed there for a year—when I arrived there were about seven members of the Party, and when I left there were about two hundred and fifty. We organized demonstrations against evictions—people couldn't pay for their homes and were being forced out. Like today, in a way—nine thousand houses have been reclaimed by FHA and the Veterans because of this Boeing thing. Then I went out into the countryside and, having been a farmer, I understood them and could talk to them and we organized lots of farmers out there.

Next, I got friendly with the Indians and I found Indians just lying down in their shacks on the bare ground dying of starvation, and I brought dozens of them into the city of Bellingham and forced the city to give them some food. The authorities hated my guts up there, but the mass of people were our friends.

This was in 1933, and I wrote an article for the Party organizer describing my Bellingham experience, the main thrust of it being that where we find local groups already carrying out a struggle on behalf of the people, we should accept and understand it and not insist that they change into "unemployment councils" under direct Party control. Well, the Party back East endorsed my attitude completely, and Alex Norell was removed and replaced by Morris Rapport, who used to say, "I am not a goddam East Coast Jew, I'm a West Coast Jew." The first time you met him you wouldn't be able to follow what he was saying because his accent was so thick, but after you came to know him you had to have enormous respect for his versatility and breadth of knowledge—I refer to the period 1935–1939 as the golden age of the Communist Party in the Northwest. . . .

During this period, Earl Browder was head of the CP in the United States, and he interpreted certain changes of policy coming from Moscow to mean that we should introduce democracy into the Party ranks instead of having everything always dictated from the top, that we should stimulate the ranks to speak up and become actively involved. In 1936, in fact, the Party was having open meetings where they would invite the public to come and observe what was going on. Once we were having a district meeting up in one of the hotels and while the President was going by in a cavalcade, being welcomed by the people outside, the national committeeman and the national committeewoman of the Democratic Party were attending our bureau meeting inside.

We really had developed enormous influence in Seattle. I was the head of the CIO at the time—I organized the CIO Council in the city in 1937 and in the state in 1938, and I was the executive secretary of it until I was ousted by John L. Lewis's henchmen who were on the move to drive Communists out of positions of power; they goon-squaded our convention and sent out a fellow by the name of J. C. Lewis to take charge.

Q.: What was the main trade of the workers you organized for the CIO?

E.V.D.: We had the longshoremen, but the CIO didn't actually organize them—the longshoremen just changed affiliation from AFL to CIO. I was in the Boatsmen's Union which traveled around the inner Sound and I persuaded them to change affiliations and we were the first on the Coast to do so. We also had a Maritime Federation in the Pacific, which was an organization of all the unions that had jurisdictional work on the water or the waterfront and we persuaded most of them to swing to the CIO. . . .

Q.: At what point did they come over to the CIO? Did you organize—

E.V.D.: I wouldn't want it said that *I* organized them—I was helping in the organization. Actually Harry Bridges was the leader of the longshoremen on the West Coast, and he made this deal with John L. Lewis to swing the longshoremen to the CIO from the AFL.

Q.: Mr. Dennett, did you serve in World War Two?

E.V.D.: Yes, and a lot of things changed while I was away. The Washington Commonwealth Federation was dissolved, the Maritime Federation was dissolved, and the Communist Party virtually dissolved during the war. It was under Browder's leadership that they changed it to the Communist Political Association instead of the Communist Party, and it developed a veneer of respectability while losing any actual efficacy.

There is another aspect of this that you probably won't believe. When I was in the army (I was married for the third time then), I got a letter from my wife informing me that she would be visited by a man who wanted her to work for him and supply him with information to aid the war effort. Her understanding of it was that it was under Roosevelt's control. I wrote back saying, hold everything until I can get home and find out what it is all about, and when I got back on furlough, the story she gave me was that this fellow was a railroad detective working for an independent federal agency which was anxious to break the bottlenecks in production —especially in some of the shipyards out here.

Well, my wife was a very knowledgeable girl, very alert, and she had a lot of connections since she was native to Seattle, and she thought she saw a good opportunity to do something really worthwhile. I told her it sounded like intelligence work, probably for the FBI, and that she should check with the Party leaders and see what they said. So she did and they said, sure, go right ahead, absolutely, we should fully cooperate with the government! So she started and they paid her seventy-five dollars a month just for submitting any information she could gather, and she did gather a good deal of critical information: she found out that one person over in the navy shipyard was a Silver Shirt leader —totally opposed to the war and doing everything he could to sabotage things. Two weeks later he was removed, and the yard started producing again. She found there were many other saboteurs and she fell into her role with considerable enthusiasm. The Party just kept telling her, you go right ahead and don't keep bothering us with questions.

About that time I had an attack of kidney stones and became disqualified for overseas assignment, and she decided to join me in the New Orleans area for a while; before she left Seattle she spoke to her contact and he said his authority had been ter-

minated, but that someone from the FBI would get
in touch with her in New Orleans. She tried to
avoid it, but they finally caught up with her. She
was working in the national Maritime Union office
and she began to hear tales of sabotage like she had
learned of up here. For instance, they were having
a terrible struggle in the shipyards in New Orleans
over the employment of Negro men alongside
white women—some people were planning fights
and there was going to be some shooting. When she
so informed the FBI, they promised to take steps to
see that there was no killing, and they organized a
big propaganda campaign and printed a big double-
page spread in the New Orleans *Item* showing black
and white workers side by side doing good work at
the plant.

But then came the Jack Decloe letter from France
complaining that the American CP had deserted its
true cause and they called a national convention to
re-establish the Party and depose Earl Browder.
Then the FBI completely changed its tune in dealing with my wife: they demanded the names of
whatever Communists were involved with the national Maritime Union—she didn't know what to
do but she ended up by giving them the best information she could get.

. . . When I got out of the service I got back to
work in Seattle at the steel mill before the time limit
—you had ninety days to get back or else you would
lose all your seniority rights. A strike had just been
settled when I arrived back in '46, and the boys
welcomed me back with open arms and elected me
secretary of the local union.

The problem that confronted them was that
Bethlehem was imposing incentive plans that the

workers didn't understand, and they didn't know what the hell to do about it. I didn't either, but I thought I could find out. I went over to the CP and . . . they said, we're too goddam busy, and offered no help of any kind. So I went out to the university . . . and the head of the math department said, look: these incentive plans aren't complicated, there's no algebra to it, you just have to be able to count 1, 2, 3, and you'll have to do that yourself.

Well, I got myself awful damn busy and I found out that I could figure out what they were doing. . . . Fortunately, I was on the grievance committee and I questioned every step that the company took with the installation of any new incentive plan: I challenged them wholesale and I incurred the enmity of the higher-ups in the union because the union was in cahoots with the company to put these plans over. They had rules there that stipulated if there was a deadlock or disagreement on the local level, the higher authorities would step in—we wouldn't have any right to settle it! I processed about fifty-five grievances in one fell swoop—I just filed a grievance against every particular part of the goddam plan.

One day a salesman came and I overheard him trying to sell them a little calculator. I was trying to figure how in the hell I was going to do all this calculation because to do it by hand was nearly impossible, so I followed the salesman out and went downtown and bought one. I still have it. Anyhow, I was able to increase our earnings by at least a third in our department when the plan was finally resolved, so the boys were all for me but the company and the international were against me.

In the meantime, the Party had proceeded to ex-

pel me because the story was circulated that I was
an FBI agent! When they confronted me with it, I
said let's get to the root of this because the top Party
leaders led my wife into it and repeatedly condoned
the whole operation. They dragged their heels and
wouldn't give me an answer, but in the few meetings we did have we almost came to physical blows.
. . . The net effect of it was that I forced the issue.
I said, I've had enough of this arbitrary dictatorship
from above; the Party is not infallible, the Party
leaders are not infallible, they continuously make
mistakes.

As a result of this, I was expelled and the Party
distributed leaflets far and wide telling everyone
that I was a renegade Trotskyite opportunist son of
a bitch, and the FBI therefore decided that this public damnation of me by the CP was really a clever
cover for the fact that I was a secret Communist
agent. The union thought I was subversive, and the
company hated my guts, and in the middle of all
this, my wife leaves me too.

Well, I developed ulcers but I was determined to
carry on the fight to the last ditch if I could, and in
fact I won the fight as far as the incentive pay was
concerned.

Then, in 1954, the House Un-American Activities
Committee subpoenaed me to appear before them
and I hired Ken MacDonald as my attorney, but
Ken was persuaded by John Coughlin [who represented the CP in most actions brought against its
members] that the only safe procedure was to in-
voke the Fifth Amendment when you appeared before the committee. However, I told Ken I had been
out of the Party for seven years—what's the statute
of limitations? He said three, and I said, all right

then, they can't prosecute me for being a member. But the real trouble you run into there is that they will ask you for names and the only way to avoid it is to plead the Fifth. So that's what I did. The first session I invoked it about eighty-seven times and I was knitting all the time, that afghan over there, and later on, socks.

When I went back to the plant between sessions, the guys there said, if you aren't ashamed of anything, if you aren't afraid of anything, why the hell don't you testify? Because if you don't, goddam it, it sounds like you're really guilty of something!

So I went back to Ken and I said, hey, I can't sell it to these guys, and the only way I can protect my job is to keep the faith with these fellows. Some of them were so angry they tried to organize a group just to escort me out of the plant—they wanted to beat me up. Ken says, well, I can arrange it, but you are taking a big risk; I said, I am taking a bigger risk if I don't.

Ken went ahead and told them I was willing to testify and they had just started taking my testimony when they said they had to adjourn. This was in June of '54, and it was March of '55 when they came back as another committee and asked me all kinds of questions—it is an enormous volume of testimony. They *did* ask me names, and I *did* name some names. But in the meantime, when they were preparing for this, I made a point to the investigator to the effect that if I named every name I knew, I was going to reveal the names of his entire information network down there—all his FBI agents and all his government agents. Did he want me to do that?

He took it up with higher authorities, and then he came back and said, you raised a very touchy ques-

tion—no one ever asked that before! You will just
have to use your judgment. So I named every damn
one of them I could think of! Some of them were
national union leaders, and they were completely
destroyed. A guy at the time who was head of the
Marine Engineers Beneficial Association I'd known
as a Party member here, and I was amazed that he'd
managed to slide so far up the line, and I had known
his brother too who was high up in the Newspaper
Guild here and I had my suspicions about him as
well. I named a hell of a lot of people and there were
a few who were very bitter about my naming them
—actually I couldn't hurt them in the least because
they were secure, longshoremen were pretty secure, nobody could hurt them because dispatching
was in control of the union. I don't think I ever
touched any employees where the company could
control the hiring.

Q.: When you named all the stooges and FBI men,
didn't you name loyal CP members too?

E.V.D.: The people I named had already been named by
Barbara Hartle, long long before. But this was the
hardest part of the experience because in a sense the
concept is that you're betraying your friends. But
you have to remember that the CP was trying to
crucify *me* by publicizing my expulsion, and I had
to fight for my own life. It was a risky thing, because it cuts you off, it isolates you from everything
you are associated with. . . .

Q.: Were you welcomed back by the company and union management?

E.V.D.: God no . . . the international set up a frame on me
in the union; it had never been a secret that I was
a Communist and read Communist literature—the
nature of the job was that you could get in quite a

lot of reading whenever you were waiting for a breakdown to be fixed and there was nothing to do but just sit there. I did a lot of knitting during those periods too. Anyway, they organized the flimsiest damn frame-up you ever heard of in your life: I was rereading Lenin's *What Is to Be Done* and a guy named Gabby came along and said, gee, that looks interesting, can I read it? And I said sure, if you want to. He kept it a long time and I had to ask him to bring it back, but he said he wasn't finished with it yet.

One day, some of the boys said, what the hell is Gabby doing in the company office, the foreman has been in there all day and all the big shots have been running in. The next thing I knew there was a union meeting and charges were preferred against me for attempting to intimidate Gabby by forcing him to read the pamphlet under the threat that I would use my influence to see that he couldn't get a job anywhere in the city! Then I had a trial, oh it was a monster, and the local union voted to remove me from office; well, the international still wasn't satisfied, so they had Gabby make an appeal to the international executive board which in turn ordered my expulsion from the union. I went to the NLRB and they said that if I made an effort to pay my dues by registered mail, they would stand by me and I couldn't be removed from my job on that account. I carried on that way for two years and finally sent a letter asking what the hell they were doing since my checks weren't being cashed or returned. About a month later all the checks came back to me, all unprocessed, and I took them to the NLRB which said, okay, to hell with it, you've done enough, you can stay in the plant. . . .

I retired from the steel mill on July 1, 1966, but my retirement wasn't adequate to live on since I still had payments to make on my house. I went to work on the waterfront as a longshore checker . . . until a year ago, January, then I took my Social Security. I was sixty-three then, and I could've taken it the year before, but I wanted to finish paying for the house, to be reasonably debt-free, and to be independent enough to do as I damn please, play golf. I represent the golf club on the model cities advisory board, and I got a little program going there that gives some of the kids in the ghetto area a chance to play and learn the game, which is otherwise almost exclusively a rich man's sport. The kids are doing quite well and it's helping us to keep the vandalism down on the golf course as well—you see it's a damn shame to see a kid sitting outside a fence looking in at a beautiful place that is forbidden to him, so what I am trying to do is to open the door.

Today, Mr. Dennett sits in his house in the southwest section of Seattle, surrounded by his impressive collection of golf trophies—strange artifacts for one who waged a lifetime battle against the spoils of capitalism.

This is Tom Beyers, of the Country Doctor Clinic:

I came to Seattle in the late spring of 1970 and within a few months was indicted for an antiwar demonstration in which fifteen thousand people blocked Interstate 5 and marched from the University District down to the City Hall and the Federal Court House, three days in a row. Fifteen thousand people taking that kind of action . . .

Q.: What was the leadership composed of?

T.B.: Predominantly college students and street people

who were organized around a nucleus of energy
that came from the East, Ithaca, who were my
friends but they preceded me and I did not necessarily agree with some of their styles. They organized
a thing called the Seattle Liberation Front. And
they led the demonstrations all of that spring. Some
of them were extremely good demonstrations and
some of them were, in retrospect, I can now say
counter-productive. At the time, I had my doubts
but the problem was that these folks had never organized working people and so they stuck to their
strong card and their strong suit which was organizing students.

Q.: But weren't there kids from the Old Left families in
that movement there?

T.B.: Sure there were. I would just like to assert that the
problem with the Seattle Liberation Front was in
its style, not in its pronouncements necessarily, but
in its style. It was much removed from what the
working class could relate to. And it was based on
the campuses; most of its actions started there. And
very little was done at the factory gates. Now the
SLF didn't try to organize unemployed people.
They took coffee down to the food lines, they distributed their leaflets, or they talked to people but
it was always talking to people, not listening to
them. . . . Cambodia was being invaded; the Chicago
people were being railroaded; there was an atmosphere of immediacy and crisis that didn't allow for
the painstaking, slow, deliberative, patient, revolutionary style that people are moving toward now.
There were very few people in for that long haul,
and that one spring half the people in the SLF
dropped out of college and became full-time organizers. But when they looked around there was no-

body that they could organize or even relate to but people like themselves. So it reached a certain peak, which was probably the freeway demonstrations after Cambodia.

Q.: When was that?

T.B.: That was May of 1970. Now by that time, eight of the people, the Seattle Eight, had already been indicted for the demonstration in February, which was before my coming. And within a month of that demonstration, I was indicted along with seven other people for forming that particular riot and rebellion. And we were not known as leaders. We were rank and file.

Q.: This was a month after your May demonstration?

T.B.: Right. So you had eight people who might be called leaders and heavies, then you had eight people who were sort of marginal to that classification and really represented the folks. And our indictment frightened people a lot worse than the first one did. Because it was a conspiracy indictment of very dubious relevance.

Q.: You were co-conspirators?

T.B.: We were a second conspiracy and the charges against us were very flimsy, but they accomplished their purpose, which was to say, this outfit, the SLF, was in for endless repression on the flimsiest of charges with the heaviest of penalties. . . .

Here's the trick. They didn't indict us for the freeway demonstration and the reason that they didn't do it is because it was too large and too popular. Fifteen thousand people were marching and we had the sympathy of a hundred thousand people. Teamsters got down out of their trucks and walked with us and parked their trucks across the lane. . . . They thought of their kids. People were dis-

gusted at Cambodia and Kent State. They couldn't
indict us for the freeway actions because half of the
town would have stood up and said, "We were
there." But there were a number of smaller demonstrations that took place on the periphery of that
action. One of them was the trashing of the ROTC
building on campus. The problem was . . .
  Q.: I know, the folks got scared when you were indicted.

A letter to *Ramparts* (May, 1972, vol. II, no. 11) sums up
what befell the Seattle Eight:

> . . . The Seattle Conspiracy charges were brought against
> eight local anti-war organizers a few months after a mili-
> tant demonstration in Seattle had erupted into violence.
> The demonstration, protesting the war in Vietnam and
> the Chicago conspiracy trial (which ended the day before
> the Seattle demonstration), was aimed at challenging the
> use of the federal courts as an instrument of political
> repression against the anti-war movement. It was broken
> up by the most violent police riot that Seattle had seen
> since the General Strike of 1919. Over 80 people were
> arrested, and some charged for doing various degrees of
> damage to the Federal Courthouse (including breaking
> some windows and throwing paint). None of the Seattle
> Conspiracy defendants were arrested at that demonstra-
> tion and no one has ever suggested that they participated
> in any violent act. But two months later they were in-
> dicted for conspiracy to break windows and (as an ironic
> twist in light of the original protest against these kind of
> charges in the Chicago case) with using the facilities of
> interstate commerce with the intent of inciting to riot—
> the infamous Rap Brown anti-riot Act. They faced ten
> years in jail.
>   The government's case was weak from the start. But

it became ludicrous when their chief witness, an FBI
informer, started to boast about his activities in "infiltrat-
ing" the Left. He told how the FBI supplied the paint to
be thrown at the Federal Courthouse and how he con-
tinually encouraged techniques of violence. Under cross-
examination by Chip Marshall, one of the defendants
who was representing himself, the informant admitted
that he hated the defendants and what they stood for so
much that he would do anything to get them into jail,
including a willingness to lie. When he was asked point
blank "You would lie?" and answered "yes," a gasp was
heard from the jury-box: the government's case looked
pretty hard to believe at this point.

Enter judicial *ex machina*. With the government's case
in tatters, the judge stepped in to save it. On the pretext
of the defendants not coming into court immediately
upon being summoned the next morning, Boldt declared
a mistrial (claiming that the defendants had prejudiced
the jury against themselves) and sent the defendants to
jail for contempt of court (6 months for this appearing 15
minutes late). The jury, now dismissed, were free to talk,
and many explained to inquiring reporters that far from
being prejudiced against the defendants, many of them
had become convinced by the FBI agent that the whole
"conspiracy" was a government set-up.

Boldt gained national prominence with his dramatic
explanation of why he was doing what he was doing. He
cited divine providence, which he said was guiding him,
and argued that it would be far better for the courts if
these kind of defendants would serve a lot of time in jail
before their trial, and the contempt sentences were a way
of getting the defendants into line. To dramatize his
action, he refused appeal bond and had the defendants
carted away to federal prisons all over the West Coast.
Five weeks later, the 9th Circuit granted bail, noting that
this misdemeanor was certainly a bailable offense since
the courts did not have the right to refuse bail even on

felony charges less than capital offenses. But Boldt had shown that he was no stickler for legal precedent or common sense. Attorney-General Mitchell and President Nixon were very appreciative of his tough sentences, and he was rewarded several months later by being named Chairman of Nixon's national Pay Board where it was hoped he would be equally tough and outrageous. . . .

Seattle's labor trouble has its roots in the split between groups that is inherent in the nature of the city. The first settlers were hard-working men, bound to succeed through the sweat of their brows. They could not comprehend people who did not want to work as hard as they did. When they found that the Indian was not working the land, they took it from him, forcing the hand of Seattle's first radical —Leschi, chief of the Nisquallis. Leschi went to war to defend his and his people's rights. He was defeated, but he left his mark on the city to be. As much, if not more so, than Chief Sealth.

As the city grew, the pioneers became businessmen and lost the time to fell the timber upon which they depended. Hired hands came into being, and in time some of these men, working in the woods or in the mills, became Wobblies. They wanted what their employers had—fancy townhouses, carriages, part of everything. The IWW offered these to them. To quote James Rowan in *The I.W.W. in the Lumber Industry,* as he presents the IWW Preamble:

The working class and the employing class have nothing in common. . . . There can be no peace as long as hunger and want are found among millions of the working people and the few, who make up the employing class, have all the good things of life.

Between these two classes a struggle must go on until the workers of the world organize as a class, take possession of the earth and the machinery of production, and abolish the wage system.

We find that the centering of the management of industries into fewer and fewer hands makes the trade unions unable to cope with the ever growing power of the employing class. The trade unions foster a state of affairs which allows one set of workers to be pitted against another set of workers in the same industry, thereby helping to defeat one another in wage wars. Moreover, the trade unions aid the employing class to mislead the workers into the belief that the working class have interests in common with their employers. These conditions can be changed and the interest of the working class upheld only by an organization formed in such a way that all its members in any one industry, or in all industries if necessary, cease work whenever a strike or lockout is on in any department thereof, thus making an injury to one an injury to all.

Instead of the conservative motto, "A fair day's wage for a fair day's work," we must inscribe on our banner the revolutionary watchword, "Abolition of the wage system."

It is the historic mission of the working class to do away with capitalism. The army of production must be organized, not only for the everyday struggle with capitalists, but also to carry on production when capitalism shall have been overthrown. By organizing industrially we are forming the structure of the new society within the shell of the old.

Seattle should have been prepared for the General Strike of 1919, yet it wasn't. While citizens panicked, the strikers went about the business of keeping the city alive. The strike collapsed as do all strikes in America, but it served notice that something was certainly wrong in Seattle.

It is difficult now, looking back, to realize completely the effect that the Red Scare had on the city of Seattle and the

State of Washington. But if one understands the fear of foreigners that Seattleites had from the very beginning, things become much clearer. Seattle has always been isolated and is so to this day, even with the perfection of modes of transportation, and this isolation, with the city perched at the very end of the frontier, has brought about some very strange states of mind among its residents. William Allen is not alone in his feelings about the beauty of living in Seattle, nor is he alone in not wanting the rest of the world to find out about it, because then Seattle would be a much bigger city than it is. Yet Allen's company, Boeing, has been primarily responsible for Seattle's accelerated growth. On the one hand is the urge to keep Seattle pure, pristine, and beautiful, a place where the good life might truly be lived. On the other is the egotism of the elite, the demand for recognition and power. WE ARE BETTER THAN SAN FRANCISCO!

Seattle's major problem is that it has tried to follow both courses at the same time. Always expanding, yet always hoping that when the expansion is completed, the undesirable elements will simply disappear. The establishment wants and needs the efforts of the labor force—how else could they hold their heads up with pride in Washington, D.C., or New York?—but they don't want them to live in the city. The laborers are still sweaty loggers, even if they've changed trades and some of them wear white collars. It would be so nice if they would simply do their jobs and leave, maybe with some sort of gigantic bussing service picking them up after work and depositing them on the other side of the Cascades, then bringing them back in time for work the next morning.

The foreign laborers have never understood their role in the scheme of Greater Seattle. So the union movements and, in reprisal, grasping at straws, the establishment and its anti-Communist mace.

Communism was an easy weapon for Seattle, because the city was still really in its infancy, already scared of the undesirable elements in its midst, when the Czar went down. People who had lived in Seattle for ten years or more became, with the General Strike of 1919, automatic pioneers because they felt in their bones that this was a much more genuine war than the one just fought in Europe. They were ripe for fear.

That's what Ole Hanson gave them. And even though Ole was publicly humiliated later, the seeds that he nurtured grew. It all had to do with the idea of the foreigner, and somehow everyone who came to Seattle without a specific invitation was considered a foreigner, and, therefore, maybe a Communist. Seattle was no safe haven for immigrants. Everyone was suspect, most particularly the laborer. A man arriving with only his skill and broken, heavily accented English was branded a Red. Ballard Swedes wanted nothing to do with the "cousins" arriving from the old country. So it was everywhere in the city; ethnic groups had become Seattleites, and any outsider was treated in the same manner. Jobs were scarce and those who held them did not want to lose them because of suspect associations.

According to management, foreign influences that refused to assimilate were trying to destroy the very fabric of American enterprise. According to the "foreign influences," all they wanted were jobs with decent pay. They couldn't get together. Somebody had to give. It was labor. Dave Beck didn't give and as a consequence grabbed hold of labor. When Beck "settled" the Newspaper Guild strike against the *Post-Intelligencer* in 1936, management lost its fear of him and looked to him as a controlling force over the rebellious laborers. No longer was it afraid of Beck's goons because worse goons had come up from the waterfront to do battle with the establishment. Labor was not so sure about the ex-laundry-truck driver, but his Teamsters had become the most powerful union in Seattle and he was able to do business with management, and so labor had to deal with him, like it or not. Hugh deLacey, Terry Pettus, and the Commonwealth Federation did and unseated Arthur Langlie for one term as governor. But that was the only real success that the left hand of the labor movement had because Beck was basically conservative—he knew which side his bread was buttered on.

One more example of a Seattle man knowing how to fit in. When, with the Red Menace, the establishment shook labor by the throat until it lay gasping, Beck walked away with an unbesmirched white collar. When it was all over, men like Terry Pettus retired to fighting battles over houseboats, and Eugene Dennett to playing golf. It took the government to get Dave Beck, because he had neglected to pay his taxes.

Foreigners kept coming in, of course, and Seattle kept growing. But by this time, it was Boeing that was bringing them in and many of them wore white collars, smelled nice, spoke well, and weren't at all the sort one would be afraid to have living next door. Not only that, these new foreigners were the responsibility of the Boeing Company, and if there were any rabble-rousers among them it was Boeing's job to weed them out.

Then the nice young professionals Boeing hired, all filled with skills and degrees and hopes, found themselves out of work, through no fault of their own, along with many of the older professionals nearing retirement age. And they had no real unions to turn to; after all, what does an engineer need a union for? They were much like their bosses —survival of the fittest; if they did their jobs well, went out and promulgated the glory of Boeing to their neighbors, they were safe. What they didn't realize was that when a crisis hits a major industry, the people at the drawing boards are often the first to go. No matter how bad things get, people are still needed to sweep floors and clean windows, even if faces are no longer there to look out of them.

The new immigrant from M.I.T. (and the older company man who had immigrated much earlier) found himself in much the same situation as the coolies brought in to drive the final railroad spikes, except no boats waited to take him back to China. And he wasn't hated, he just wasn't needed.

Jack Driscoll, director of the Emergency Employment Agency, says:

> I think our economy is a growing economy. I think the gain for profit is still a basic motivation for most people and unless everybody gets into that bag, it's fairly difficult for you as an individual. I think the turnaround for someone who has been working at Boeing living east of the lake, that for him to decide that he is suddenly going to give that all up and accept a whole new life style, it is impossible. They are not ready for it. I don't know how many have. And I would suggest that those who have may be happier but I bet you there are more who haven't and have no interest at all in giving it up.
>
> Q.: What if they are not willing to accept a $12,000 salary after $18,000, and this is understandable, and yet there isn't any $18,000 job for them. What are they going to do? Is welfare or going to the food bank better?
>
> J.D.: Some of them feel that collecting unemployment is better.
>
> Q.: But that's a very temporary state of affairs.
>
> J.D.: The whole idea is that if they accept a position for less money . . .
>
> Q.: It goes down on their résumés.
>
> J.D.: That's right. And when they go out looking for

another job, in their résumé it says that they worked for the city of Seattle as assistant analyst for $900 a month and that really is hard.

Still, all in all, I think Seattle is a comfortable place. I remember reading in a tavern I went to once, it said it is a big city with a small mind. I think people are fairly provincial. I don't know if Seattle is going anywhere or not now. I think it is frozen right now. I think the economy has just stifled almost anything in Seattle. It is very difficult to think progressive or think future for a lot of people when they have the immediate problems that they are faced with. So it is kind of hard to relate to today's Seattle in terms of "if you knew how it was in '68." When I look at the unemployment rate then, it was 2.8 percent. A fairly vibrant community. I think it is still moving. Seattle is a city and I think it is an outstanding place to be . . . if you have a job.

Of the new unemployed, however, just about all are aerospace. I think that is one of the problems that we're not very happy about; certainly I feel vets, particularly those who served in Vietnam, deserve every break in the world. But the EE Act is such that it kind of forces you into one position, saying serve all of these significant segments based on their rate of unemployment and they give you forty percent veteran priority. Well, that means someone is going to end up holding the short end of the stick and the big number are going to be those who have been unemployed for a long time—the minorities and disadvantaged. Women are not included at all in the significant segments of the population.

Something has to be done, though. Boeing is never going to get back to 110,000. That economist from Bell Tel made some projections and I think he still had us around eight percent in 1980 if things don't change. The only answer is increase industry in Seattle, otherwise you can't depend upon everyone being employed by the government. The octopus is fairly big now—we don't need people bumping into each other. Increased industry and more jobs for private enterprise is the only answer to the real ills of Seattle.

· That's what happens to labor when it forgets that it is mere labor. Give him a degree, a nice suit, pat him on the back, and he thinks he's important. Not a hired hand, but part of the club. He's been given a real inside glimpse of the world of power. Once that happens you know you can't be fired. You hustle for the company wherever you go. You vote the company line and, although it's not called party line, you know full well it is. There are Boeing Senators, Boeing Congressmen, and Boeing city councilmen, and you vote for them and encourage others to vote for them because they are your people. Workers and bosses look the same, just as they did in the early days, and Seattle is forced to learn the same lesson all over again, only this time on a much grander scale.

Self-help programs in Seattle, such as SEAVEST, Talent Plus, and Start-Up sprouted up across the city. The object of all of these organizations was to find jobs for the unemployed, and they were manned by the unemployed, but there is a difference between organizing on the job and trying to organize once the job is dead. SPEA, the engineers' union at Boeing, was very ineffective. No one really wanted to join it because no one felt the need. They had been offered security and needed no group action. The International Association of Machinists and Aerospace

Workers, the dominant union at Boeing, had a little better luck, but not much.

This is how John Gillingham, labor economist and negotiator, explained the labor picture:

> The key question is not whether there is something peculiar about Boeing in respect to union and management relations but rather why is the airframe industry not an industry in which the unions have been able to generate great strength? Well, there are two or three reasons I would mention that are very important. The first is that it's an industry that grew up very rapidly; in the area around World War Two, something like fifty thousand planes were ordered, an impossible number, and these workers were recruited from all over the country, including lots of women and lots of people from the boondocks and inaccessible nonurban areas—people without any history of industrial employment or unionism.
>
> Secondly, this labor force is in the main a semi-skilled labor force—the production workers. Now it's true you've got a very high proportion of technicians and professionally trained people like the engineers, but they have always held themselves apart from unionism, and they still do—the reason SPEA charges dues of only fifty to seventy-five cents a month is because they have a tough time keeping even fifty percent of the engineers in it. Because the engineers believe that merit is what you progress on and they choose to operate on that basis—they decline to get involved with a standard rate for everybody. This was the largest union of engineers in the country, but they never drove after the kinds of objectives you normally associate with unions; in

fact, SPEA's number-one objective was to prevent a compression in the wage scale by making sure that the amount by which Boeing had to increase its entering wage for young engineers each year was transmitted throughout the whole wage structure. At any rate, that takes care of the engineers.

Well, once you get a group of skilled mechanics, machinists, and tool-and-die workers and so forth, the bulk of these production workers are what might be called semiskilled: they are operators. And these people are not always material for a militant and tough kind of union organization. Or at least it takes them some time—and then they have to be in advantageous bargaining positions. It takes an experience like the auto workers had through the twenties and thirties to develop that kind of bitterness and hostility and sense of common cause against your employer that permitted the emergence of the auto workers after twenty years of very tough times.

But the point here is that these operators don't have the intrinsic bargaining power that skilled people do—*it's easy to replace such people.* When the big Boeing postwar strike occurred in 1948, Boeing began to recruit employees to replace those on strike, and it re-employed something like four thousand people from among its own former employees —they came right across their own picket line to go back to work! People realized not only how easily they could be replaced but, in addition, the company began to reduce its ranks very substantially from peak production almost to zero—and that tends to take most of the enthusiasm out of a strike: people begin to wonder who is going to be able to stay on at the job.

Finally, and this is very important in American labor relations, these people did not have any strong sense of common cause or solidarity—they were from Illinois, Louisiana, and God knows where else.

Anyway, in '48, what caused the company to take the strike more than any other factor was that they had to get rid of a seniority provision which I think was a kind of mistake on both sides—I mean, here they are reducing personnel by great numbers and a man has seniority in Department A but that's being closed out and he can displace somebody in Department B and that guy can displace someone in D and he's got seniority over someone in C and so forth and you might have seventeen moves over one layoff and also lose the opportunity to demonstrate who can do the job. It was an impossible kind of system, and the union leadership couldn't really defend it either; so negotiations for a new agreement dragged on in a desultory way through '47, but in '48, a group of union people who were critics of the incoming officers began to advocate a strike, saying the goddam company is stalling us out and meanwhile our rights are going down the drain, and before the leadership knew it, there was a sudden swell here for a strike and they felt they could not oppose it successfully without discrediting themselves in the eyes of the rank and file. They made a fatal mistake as it turns out: they did not give sixty days' notice as the Taft-Hartley Act required, and the union lost its status as bargaining representative.

At that time the union was trying to press an unfair labor practice charge against the company because of alleged favoring of the Teamsters, who began organizing these forty thousand people behind the Machinists' picket line—Beck took the position that to strike under these circumstances and for these issues was suicide and the Teamsters even set up a hiring hall, sort of like an employment agency, and they'd recruit people looking for work, sign them up, and send them over to the company, who would hire them on as Teamsters.

Well, the Machinists beat the Teamsters; the Machinists organized its members again over the next eighteen months—Beck's Cadillacs and tailor-made suits rubbed people the wrong way—and petitioned the NLRB to hold an election and they won a majority; they were the official bargaining representatives once again. But the company won the strike, and the Machinists went back with greatly reduced ranks and with no contract. There just never was a relevant kind of solidarity in that labor force. Because it's an up and down industry—whenever you are really not sure about your job next year you are more concerned about security considerations.

Q.: This is the very same labor force that the people from Boeing told me had such a high turnover rate from people quitting and having to be replaced? How does that fit in with the profile?

J.G.: Those who *want* to stay on are apprehensive about job security, but there are many who don't see themselves spending their life with Boeing—these are people without big investments in their jobs, people not permanently committed to the labor force but who are helping to pay off a car or a divorce fee or something like that, and they are not willing to get out there on the picket line and get hit over the head or hit somebody else and really tighten up and see that scabbers don't get in there.

That's part of what I call this heterogeneous, low-level, industrialized kind of labor force—it's not like steel where you have three generations of steelworkers who in the main never worked anywhere else. When Boeing expands, it recruits from rural towns, and when business contracts, those who don't have roots here or skills that are readily transferred just pull up stakes and go, and as for the women, daughters and wives tend to be more peaceful than militant.

All of these factors account for less solidarity on the union side, together with the fact that the airframe industry has been subject to such tremendous fluctuations and demands that it suffers a chronic sort of uncertainty. Take, for instance, the last eight years: a rising economy, starting in about 1965, saw the demand for civilian flight rising spectacularly and the big contest of who is going to get in there first with the next big plane—if you don't get the 747 out *now* Lockheed will take the lead, and once Northwest gets it Pan American has to have it and so on. So the 747 turns out to be a profitable thing and causes a great deal of expansion plus a defense expansion which had not been anticipated and Boeing suddenly has this terrific lift and starts scouring the country for people—they went up from fifty thousand to a hundred thousand employees in three years. Then comes the economic crunch and the rate at which airlines were ordering 747s was cut down to almost nothing because they couldn't finance them, and the Defense Department cuts back and, most of all, NASA cuts back. So here we have the three major sources of aerospace going simultaneously, and the latter two, Defense and NASA, probably permanently, and the airframe in-

dustry had no control over it at all. Suddenly, here
are a hundred thousand people with nothing to do.
So they came down, of course; in less than two years
they were headed for thirty-two thousand. Well,
that's not the kind of industry where you can build
a good, solid, unionized work force, especially when
there's so much differentiation within it—engineers and professional people here and a group of
skilled workers there with quite different interests
from the rank and file.

Anyway, what kind of compelling forces could
they exert on management? In a case like we've
been talking about, what could you even do about
production? Strike to maintain more people on the
payroll? To protest the firing of certain kinds of
engineers while they hired others? What kind of
pressure could they put on the company? The answer is, not very much.

Not very much.

Nobody in America stays where he wants to, unless he
controls the place. That is the secret that everyone must
know when he discovers a good job and a beautiful house.
It is his only for a while.

For the "de-hired" white-collar worker who refuses to
leave Seattle, there are several options. One is to try to wait
it out, using the savings, selling the car, having the wife and
children get jobs. Another is to try to grab anything that
is available, cab-driving, the post office, part-time bartend-
ing. The third is to try one of the self-help programs,
SEAVEST, or Talent Plus. Although each of these programs makes claims for its unique effectiveness, they are all
basically the same. They are formed by and for out-of-work
aerospace professionals, particularly those let go by Boeing, and they try to do many different but supposedly inter-

locking things; still, they seem to have a common focus, the résumé (that all-important piece of paper that either saves a man or makes him a fool)—how to do it, how to show your bright side; how to recycle old skills into new talents that will make you more appealing in today's market.

Here is a SEAVEST volunteer:

> We're eleven hundred strong in the State of Washington. SEA stands for Self-help Employment Association, the VEST stands for Volunteer Engineers, Scientists, and Technicians, but we're not all Boeing people. We are here to find ourselves a job and at the same time—in order to join our organization—we agree to go through a little workshop to learn how to write a résumé and how to be an interviewee. The second thing you must do is put in eight hours a week, and the third thing is you must attend our weekly meetings for one hour in the morning, because this is how we communicate with each other. Any new jobs that come, any new schools that we have added. This makes us different from any of the others. You mentioned this paranoid thing. Sure we have it—I think you're bound to be paranoid if you're unemployed—and it helps to see others who are just as badly off as you.

And things are hardly different next door at Talent Plus:

> A.: A number of us laid-off Boeing engineers and administrative people organized Talent Plus in the latter part of 1970, and as the year progressed we built up the membership from various areas of endeavor—sales people, for instance. We have about fifty percent success in placing people.
> Q.: How many would you say you have dealt with?

A.: About three hundred people have come through Talent Plus.

Q.: And you've found permanent jobs for a hundred and fifty of them?

A.: Well, no, I couldn't say that *we* have placed them . . . we have helped them place themselves.

Q.: How many of those have had to relocate out of Seattle?

A.: I would say ten—not many more.

Q.: Out of the remaining hundred and forty, how many have been placed in engineering positions or in jobs commensurate with what they previously held, and how many have had to go into entirely new fields?

A.: Most of them have had to go into other fields.

Q.: Of those still unemployed, how many are on welfare?

A.: We have had only one member on welfare—but that is probably due to the fact that most of them are ineligible for assistance.

Q.: How do the others support themselves?

A.: Unemployment insurance and life savings.

Q.: How many have exhausted their unemployment benefits?

A.: Most of them.

Q.: Had you ever been laid off by Boeing before?

A.: Yeah, twice before.

Q.: That didn't discourage you from going to work for them again?

A.: No. If you don't rock the boat, they take you on again, and they pay pretty good. You get spoiled.

Q.: May I ask what your name is, sir?

A.: I'd just as soon not say.

Bill Brammer, an ex-Boeing technical writer, is someone who just as soon would say:

Q.: What do you think of Talent Plus?

B.B.: I guess I got turned off of them early in the game. The first thing I could see was these guys were just so damn busy crying on each other's shoulders— sort of like Alcoholics Anonymous.

Q.: They weren't trying to develop jobs?

B.B.: Not at first. Later they made some inroads in this direction, but I was at a point where I had been unemployed for two years with four kids at home —and I needed a lot more than friendly commiseration. I needed some refreshing help, some news about jobs—different kinds of jobs.

Q.: You are employed now with Start-Up?

B.B.: Yes. I heard about it through a friend who arranged to have me trained for the position. Start-Up began in 1971, when unemployment peaked. We're sponsored by United Way, but it was conceived by Mike McManus whose goal was to help unemployed people—not just professionals—get *all* the kinds of counseling an unemployed person needs, instead of being sent from agency to agency. Marriage counseling, drug counseling, financial counseling, where to get food, how to get assistance. We try to have as many different services under one roof as possible.

Q.: How did you manage before you got this job?

B.B.: I used up my unemployment benefits and all the resources we had. And there was a hell of a period of harassment from our creditors. As I mentioned earlier, I had borrowed about a thousand dollars from the Boeing Company [the Boeing Credit Union—not officially part of Boeing] to put a roof on my house. After I was laid off, they actually started sending me these dunning letters with red borders. I got so mad I borrowed money from someplace else

just to pay Boeing off. Paid them off to get them the
hell out of my hair. We were completely wiped out.

Those in their fifties whose professional experience has
been in one narrow groove in an industry that now regards
them as obsolete can perhaps qualify for one of the handful
of retraining programs offered at some of the universities
in the area. Burt Laird speaks:

Q.: What was your job title at Boeing?
B.L.: I was in middle management from about 1955.
Q.: Had you ever been laid off before?
B.L.: No, I have never experienced anything like this
before.
Q.: When did it happen?
B.L.: In the summer of 1970.
Q.: Did you have notice?
B.L.: Oh, a matter of three or four weeks. A lot of us
could see it coming, though—there were signs of it
as early as 1968. . . . I sort of had the suspicion that
sooner or later we might have to experience a period of retrenchment and that people would have to
be let go. But I had been with them for almost
nineteen years, and I enjoyed the work—you figure
you just have to hang on and hope.
Q.: What happened when you were let go?
B.L.: Boeing had a savings program wherein if you contributed a certain percent, they would match it and
invest it for you. Of course at that same time the
stock market was going down too, so your savings
weren't worth what they had been earlier. In my
case, it wasn't a very large amount. I guess we were
a typical conservative couple; we have no children,
we had saved a little bit, and with what we had in

the bank and unemployment benefits, we have been able to hang on. But time is running out now, and it looks like we will have to put our home on the market.

Q.: You still owe mortgage payments?

B.L.: Oh yes. Well, in July I enrolled in this program at the University of Washington. It's under the Department of Labor which gave the National Society of Professional Engineers a contract to make a study of possible industry areas where aerospace engineers, scientists, technicians could utilize their expertise with a certain amount of retraining. The areas that looked most promising turned out to be power companies and utilities, because of the so-called energy crisis about to descend on us, and the food industry and the construction industry. The one I'm in has to do with food. Designing processing equipment.

Q.: How long is the course?

B.L.: This particular one I'm attending runs about twelve weeks. They pay a sustenance and each dependent is five dollars a month additional. It about equals unemployment insurance.

Q.: And then do they try to place you within the area?

B.L.: Well, the chances of getting a food industry job in this area are pretty far down the scale, but they send your résumés to a number of food-related companies and equipment manufacturers, and also to the Food and Drug Administration.

Q.: How long have you owned your own home?

B.L.: Since coming to Seattle in 1950. When Boeing was beginning to build.

Q.: Could you tell me a little about the emotional changes you have been through? Did you feel it was a personal reflection on you when you first were fired?

B.L.: Yes, I went through a lot of conversations with myself: what in the blazes did I do wrong over the years to warrant being laid off? What should I have done differently? It's an experience I wouldn't want to ever go through again, but I think my values have changed. I realize what a paper foundation so much of our economic structure is built on, money being an eternal growth factor which it can't be. So many people don't understand this. For example, in our class at the U most of the fellows think this is just a temporary situation, and they regard this retraining as just sort of treading water until they get rehired in their old jobs again. . . .

Q.: Has it been very difficult on your wife, this period?

B.L.: Very much so. She has had a terrific adjustment to make. She couldn't find a job because she is my age and did not work for quite a number of years.

Q.: Have your politics changed in any way?

B.L.: Oh, I never have been politically oriented. I've always felt our political system leaves a lot to be desired. It is nothing but compromise and I'm a firm believer that things have to be planned and laid out—at least a number of alternatives studied and explored—and we don't have that in our unplanned let's-get-it-while-we-can power structure, with little or no regard for the toll this takes on our natural resources, or on people. . . .

Q.: What do you think the solution would be for the aerospace industry?

B.L.: Well, perhaps the United States could utilize a system like the Japanese have. They more or less have a lifelong job with a particular company, and when

they reach retirement age they either receive benefits or a lump sum. They don't have to worry about
layoffs or unemployment: when things are good,
everyone shares the profit, and they also share the
burden when things aren't. Even at Boeing, I took
a pay cut to stay on for several months at the end.

The last resort for an engineer who can't get into a recy-
cling program may be a nonengineering job in the public
sector—despite the fact that the job may be totally inappro-
priate for his training, temperament, and talent. This is
what happened to John Conroy:

Q.: How long did you work for Boeing?
J.C.: Just eleven years.
Q.: How many children do you have?
J.C.: Nine.
Q.: Are you over forty-five?
J.C.: Oh, you bet!
Q.: Had you ever been laid off before?
J.C.: Yes, it was not a brand-new experience for me.
Q.: The last time, how long were you out of work?
J.C.: Six months. That was 1958, just prior to my coming
    out to Boeing. I had worked for the Brunswick Cor-
    poration in Michigan and they had reorganizational
    layoffs and budgetary layoffs.
Q.: When were you laid off at Boeing?
J.C.: February, 1970. I was essentially unemployed for
    the next two years, exhausted all my unemploy-
    ment insurance, and then I got on the emergency
    program with the State Highway Department. I
    was learning to be a surplus property agent and
    had finished about three months of it when there
    was an opportunity that came along with the

State Health Department on another emergency
program [the Emergency Employment Act].
That is the one I'm working on now—as a hotel
inspector. It pays only half what I earned at
Boeing—and that's after a two-year period of essentially no income.

Q.: What did you do during this time? Did you liqui-
date any assets, like a second car—

J.C.: I don't have a second car. We barely have a first.

MRS. C.: We just never buy anything. We've been living on
food stamps.

J.C.: If it wasn't for the food stamps, we would have
been totally devastated because we would have
had to use what little money there was for food.
We couldn't have made our payments on the
house, for example.

MRS. C.: Our children go to parochial school, so they wear
uniforms. Clothes weren't a problem, but medical
and dental bills were. The Model Cities program
picked up those bills this past year—it was a big
help because previously the kids weren't getting
any dental care at all. . . .

Q.: Did you have any savings?

J.C.: I had some credit in the Boeing pension fund, and
some credit accrued from unused sick leave.

Q.: Can you withdraw anything from the pension
fund when you are laid off?

J.C.: Only parts of it. I have forgotten what the figures
are. You see, as long as you remain on layoff status,
you retain some pension eligibility. If you resign,
you lose it completely, and if you refuse the job or
the salary they want you for when they call you
back—either because the money is much less than
you were making, or because the job seems totally

unsuitable for you—you have removed yourself from layoff status and forfeited your pension fund eligibility.

Q.: Let me ask you for your opinion on a number of questions. When I learned that Boeing was recruiting from the outside again I said to Bill Allen [then head of Boeing]: Don't you feel that you should retrain engineers who are laid off and live in the area before bringing in a new crop of engineers? And he said, first of all, retraining is too expensive, takes too much time, and isn't very effective. If I have the teachers to retrain others, I might as well be using the teachers themselves. I said, don't you feel you owe an obligation to those you hired, and who have worked for you for a considerable span of years? Haven't you heard, he answered, of survival of the fittest?

I told him that one ex-engineer had mentioned a system in Japan whereby workers are hired for life. . . . Mr. Allen said it wouldn't work in this country —people are too lazy. If they knew they had that security, they wouldn't work; and anyway, an employer in a free enterprise system has to be able to get the best for the least. If one worker is being inefficient, you have to be allowed to get rid of him. I said, I guess that means hiring newer, younger ones who will work for less than if you had to rehire the older ones. He said, yes, that's what is meant by survival of the fittest. Management's job is to show a profit. What do you think about this?

J.C.: Well, I think that a certain amount of that security which Mr. Allen is criticizing is a very definite necessity—particularly for the older person. On the other hand, I don't personally like the loss of freedom to change from one job to another, from one

company to another. But his idea of the fittest surviving is nonsense—very often the ones who sur-
vive are simply those who blow smoke rings around
everybody, they're really dead wood who are good
at ingratiating themselves with some particular
people or group. . . .

Q.: I understand Boeing is now recruiting electrical
engineers. Could you be retrained for that kind of
work?

J.C.: Absolutely. My background bears this out: my degree is as a chemist—I am not a materials engineer
by virtue of training or education. I am a materials
engineer because I was a chemist who got involved
in materials engineering, and my chemistry was the
backbone for my work in the same way as my
materials engineering could become the backbone
of my work as an electrical engineer.

Q.: Aside from financial hardships, has your being laid
off had any marked effect on the children?

J.C.: I do think they suffered through discussions at
school, you know, why isn't your father still
working, and things like that. At one point my
seventh-grader came home and said they had had
an economist at school who claimed that any
man who had been unemployed for six months
would never get a job again for the rest of his
life. Another thing is the attitude of Seattle people on Boeing. They think anybody that Boeing
imports, well, we're better off rid of them. Many
people won't hesitate to tell you that.

For other out-of-work professionals who don't get into
emergency employment programs (and who may not have
beneficent neighbors), welfare is the court of last resort—
but even here the necessary assistance often is not forth-

coming because of complex eligibility requirements. Wayne Nelson of Legal Services Center explains:

> Over the past two years, during this cutback at Boeing, there has been a steady progression of more restrictive eligibility regulations in this state. When Evans [Dan Evans, governor of Washington] can say in February that the welfare rolls are down because of greater administrative efficiency or more aggressive fraud control, they are really down because category after category of recipients are being systematically cut off. And they don't do it in massive ways, they do it in small, fastidious ways: you cut off eighteen-year-olds who are still in high school who previously got assistance. You cut them off and it saves so many millions of dollars. You cut back on the medical care because medical care represents thirty-five percent of the welfare budget in this state. They cut back so welfare recipients can only have one visit per month to a doctor. They can't get dental work where before they could. They can't get eyeglasses unless they fall down in the street. That's where the state saves money. They cut back on grants by imposing a maximum amount that large families can receive. . . . And when Employment Security reports a decrease in unemployment, you find that this is attributable to the fact that increasing numbers of people have exhausted their benefits rather than to the fact that increasing numbers of people have gone out and found work. Then of course there are many people who aren't covered at all—farm workers, migrant workers, domestics, and so on.

Q.: What kind of reforms are you looking to effect?

W.N.: That's really hard to say. The whole system has got

to go and be replaced by a guaranteed minimum income. For example, welfare itself rises and falls, case loads and money grants rise and fall with the political mood. If things are going bad, you pit welfare recipients against working people and you say these recipients are parasites on your honest paycheck—and why should some people work and others not? Well, why not? We have more people than jobs anyway. If you give people enough to satisfy their basic necessities, say with a guaranteed income of $6,500, you can eliminate all these funky programs that are supposed to take up the slack. And if there are some who don't want to work for enough to survive, let them not work but let them survive. . . .

Q.: What are the eligibility requirements for nonassistance food stamps?

W.N.: There are some pretty strict assets—$1,500 for persons under sixty-five, $3,000 if you are over sixty-five, and then they have a lot of incredibly restrictive regulations to keep certain people from getting the stamps. For instance, when they started in April, they had a provision that if one person was unrelated to any other person in a household, the whole household was ineligible. It was clearly written to ban communes. But suppose a migrant family took in some little child whose parents had deserted him—the whole family would be ineligibile for food stamps. So we got that reversed. They had another little goodie called the tax dependent clause. If you are eighteen years of age or older and someone else who is not receiving food stamps claims you as a tax dependent, you and the whole household you live in are ineligible to participate in the food stamp program during the year you were

claimed as an exemption, and for one year there-
after. That was written with college students in
mind. Well, we have all of these welfare mothers
whose husbands are gone but were paid a minimum
support; they paid out more than half of their support for one of their children—and thus are claiming those children as tax dependents. So now these
mothers can't get food stamps. It's illogical, puni-
tive. In dealing with the welfare system—and I have
been dealing with it for a long time—you are dealing with a system that is imposing some sort of
moral value on the people it services. On whom you
can live with, on what you can do. . . . Eligibility
means, very basically, that you are dividing people
up into classes, categories, judging who is fit to sur-
vive.

Seattle has always been abhorrent of welfare, not because
eligibility requirements were too restrictive but because
everyone was expected to provide for himself, to fend for
himself. According to Arthur Denny, who was not speaking for himself alone, there was little or no time for leisure
or sport. Men were expected to work, eat, and sleep, with
the major portion of the day taken up by the first. In that
respect they were not so very different from their ancestors
who landed at Plymouth. (It is only fitting that a piece of
Plymouth Rock was deposited like a transplant on Alki
Point in 1926. It showed the fulfillment of a nation's dreams.
The continent was finally conquered.) But the motives behind the stern work ethic differed vastly between the two
groups of settlers. The Plymouth pilgrims fought for survival when they landed; they had no real notion of the
vastness of the wilderness that faced them. That is why
they kept their eyes tight to the ground, holding on, for a
while at least, to a tiny corner. The Seattle pilgrims had the

lesson of profit. If they struggled for survival, they knew that eventually the place they had picked for their own would bring them a harvest of money. They looked back at the land they had left, not with fear or loathing but with the knowledge that in some way the land they held would yield value and make them rich men—"We were all Capitalists in those days."

On what seemed to be the final frontier of America, there was no room for a lazy man. One worked as hard as he could and there was always room for an able, diligent body. So long as one followed rules. It was inconceivable for someone to be indigent, out of work, or down on his luck. Downright sinful.

Remember, though, that Seattle was an American afterthought, born to middle-aged parents who thought that their child-rearing days were over. It was just learning to walk while the Civil War was being fought, still being bottle fed when the Klondike strike hit, and barely in knee pants when World War I and the shipyards came into their own.

How can a child deal with people who are out of work, not because they want to be but because there are no jobs? All he can do is whine. This is what happened to Seattle, suddenly. Without preparation the city was forced to deal with unemployed residents. And it didn't like it one bit.

Some people say that the failure of the General Strike of 1919 destroyed any possibility of unity in the labor movement. Maybe it did. But it also pointed to one error that the founding fathers of the city had never considered (and are still fighting over to this day): if you lure people to a place with the promise of work and allow them to settle and then the work disappears, those who did the luring have a responsibility to those who bit on the bait. They cannot simply be asked to leave, to emigrate. Granted it's distasteful to have a bunch of sluggards hanging around on the dole while you're still working hard trying to save your fortune, but the one who asked cannot say, "Who asked you to come in the first place?"

By 1919 everybody knew.

Not that Seattle turned around and did flip-flops for the indigents who seemed to be stuck there, but at least the solid citizens realized that the back-of-the-hand technique wasn't working. The city was scared by the Communists in its midst and desperate for responsible leadership. It knew it was in trouble and, probably more than any other American city, needed the 1920s, "the Coolidge prosperity years," to quote Terry Pettus, to calm things down for a while.

People still went hungry, but political action seemed to be separated from poverty. Dead, in fact. Greed still ran rampant, but some sores were allowed to heal, or at least form temporary scabs. The Depression and the Roosevelt years that followed changed all that.

Seattle went head-on into a welfare-state crisis that has yet to be resolved.

It is easy to blame the Boeing Company for Seattle's ills —it did shuck off more than seventy thousand people—but the welfare problems in Seattle go back much farther than Boeing's booms and busts. Once there was a time when a broke and beaten David Denny could turn his back on the city and walk out to the woods of Washelli. Washelli is now a cemetery, and Seattle residents cannot walk far enough to escape failure or disdain.

Welfare in Seattle began with the elderly. When Seattle was an infant, there was no problem with senior citizens. Older people might have been laborers, but the land they worked was theirs. As the town edged its way into becoming a city, by sudden starts and stops, people began living on land they didn't own and as they grew older they had no money. They had to be taken care of. Seattle and the State of Washington faced the issue of old-age pensions.

But that was only the tip of the iceberg.

Seattle has always seemed to thrive on catastrophes. The great fire cleaned up the downtown area. The Klondike strike, dragging broken dreams like flotsam, put the city on the nation's maps. World War I brought the illusion of permanent prosperity. World War II turned the Boeing Company into a monster of industry. Sputniks, missile gaps, bigger and faster commercial transports, the SST, on and on. And Seattle found herself with more and more people who could not afford to live there and yet would not be thrown out.

Mike McManus, who has constructed a number of self-guidance and workshop programs for the unemployed, says:

> The unemployed person, he does not blame the big B. He is angry and resentful at the big B because he knows who is left. But he says I must have screwed up. I am the failure because I am not there and my friends are there. And I don't want to be around unemployed people because it is too embarrassing. And so I don't want to be a part of your militant radical organization because that's like being back down at the breadline. As a matter of fact I don't even want to go to Employment Security for an unemployment check because I don't want to play that game. I work for what I get. I don't want any goddam handouts. So it is a constituency that really ain't there because nobody will identify themselves as being part of that constituency. They are victimized by the various systems, but they are ashamed to say so.

Ken Baxter is warehouse manager of Neighbors in Need Food Bank:

Q.: I read that when you opened you had about thirty-seven food banks and you were feeding an average of twenty thousand people a week and I now know that you have curtailed the operation. How many banks do you have?

K.B.: We have about twenty-five, and we haven't curtailed the number of people.

Q.: Do you think it has gone up?

K.B.: No. It seems to have leveled off. In the beginning of the month, it will run in the vicinity of ten thousand to twelve thousand or maybe a little more than that. Toward the end of the month—well, a week ago Friday we made a fairly accurate check of the number of families that we give food to and it ran about ten thousand people on one day.

Q.: How many days a week are you open?

K.B.: We are open two days a week now.

Q.: Do you think you would have the same ten thousand on the second day or do you think it is a different group?

K.B.: Well, to a certain extent we get different people. However, there will be a certain amount who come on the second day. We are open on Monday and Friday so we plan our distribution a week or so in advance. I am sending out orders for Friday now and I am basing my estimate on eight thousand to nine thousand. So it will run somewhere near fifteen thousand during the week. And then toward the end it will run more. Maybe as high as twenty thousand.

Q.: Why does it increase toward the end of the month?

K.B.: We have, well, you can take the people that we serve who need food and roughly divide them into three groups. The first group is the people who are of employable age who are unemployed.

Q.: So that first group that is employable but unemployed is not eligible for welfare, only for unemployment insurance.

K.B.: That's right. But so many of those unemployment
benefits have expired. At the present time and for
the past several weeks we have had quite a few who
have recently been unemployed by Lockheed and
by Todd Shipyards. Now, you have heard very little about them. The media people are giving so little
publicity to the problem of the unemployed, but
just as soon as the statistics of the unemployed are
dropped a small fraction of a percentage point, well,
that makes headlines. They don't say anything
about it when it goes up. . . .

The second tangible group would be those who
are receiving some kind of welfare benefits. Many
of those are not of employable age. Say they are
women who are supporting small children with
Aid to Dependent Children. . . . There are many
older people in that group who are only receiving
small allowances or allotments, and the nature of
their needs are particularly for health, and they
arise as a result of the fair allowances being very
substantially reduced several years ago. And also
they have enough to support themselves during the
first half of the month but then you see the number
of people drops when the checks come out. Toward
the end of the month we get a substantial number
of people. . . .

Then the third group would be those who are
very closely related to the second group. They are
on Social Security, pensions (which are relatively
small), and find that they are just unable to live on
it a month so they are just about like the welfare
recipients.

Now in the case of both the second and the third groups, there are those who, for one reason or the other, their pension checks have been delayed or lost, or who have made application and are still waiting for it. We had a case this morning that I think is a classic example of those who fit into this category. A woman called a couple of hours ago. The tone of her voice was desperate and she wanted to know where she could get some food. She said that she was hungry. She was a widow, whose husband had died a couple of years ago. She has made application for welfare, but it still takes a lot of time for it to be processed. The only thing she has eaten in the last three days is bread; and so she was desperately in need of food. Just parenthetically, we maintain an emergency food bank right next door here to handle cases like this because the food banks are open on Monday and Friday and that means during the week, for the people who have an emergency need, the food banks are closed. So we maintain an emergency food bank where the case workers or the people who are referred to us can call, and they have someplace to go and get the food.

Who could have dreamed that "it" would happen to Seattle? Only the cynic looking with jaundiced eyes on the perfection of modern America at the turn of the century in beautiful Seattle would have the gall to say that things were not what they seemed to be: that something like Neighbors in Need would ever have to come into being.

It all did happen, with micro-steps, as the city began to realize itself. Despite disclaimers, Seattle came of age and was confronted by the fully grown ogre it had feared all along. People who lived in Seattle could not afford to live there, yet they could not and would not move. They had to be cared for.

Jon Stewart, a free-lance writer, went to Seattle to research a book on the "new poor." In an article published in *Ramparts* magazine in May, 1972, he summed up his feelings:

> The day I left Seattle a heavy snowfall had blanketed the city under a foot of snow. Children, out of school, were skiing and sledding in the streets, and the few cars on the road were sliding and skidding hopelessly. Most businesses downtown had announced they wouldn't open at all, and all government offices were closed for the day. The Boeing Company by mid-morning announced over the radio that all plants would be closed. Seattle had come to a white, cold, glistening standstill.
>
> Inside the Seattle-Tacoma Airport terminal a sign gave credence to my last visual impression of the city. It read, "Will The Last Person Leaving Seattle Please Turn Out The Lights."

Earlier in the article, Stewart tried to deal with the Boeing-Seattle "problem":

> When the statistics come off the printed page and take on flesh and blood, what emerges in Seattle is, to a considerable extent, something other than the traditional, down and out, unskilled, hard-core unemployed. Not that they don't exist in legion number, but alongside them are the ranks of highly skilled, educated, middle-income families. The 67,000 Boeing workers who have been laid off since late 1968 have not packed their bags and fled the holocaust as many had hoped. To a surprising extent, they've stayed on.

Seattle is not a traditional American city. It is much easier to understand welfare looking at New York, where the city belongs either to the very rich or the very poor. It is also easy to look at welfare as a gift to the hard-core unemployed, people who have never worked and, so the givers feel, never will. It is much more difficult to look at lines of people at food banks (lined up three to four hours before the banks open to make sure they get something before the food runs out) wearing the remnants of thirty years of training and hard work.

The charms of the city are also its undoing. Its eternal optimism and foolish naïveté draw people and keep them like flies caught in a spider's web. Seattle cannot tell its unemployed to go home, because they are home.

The carnival-like, on-the-go atmosphere of Seattle hides its poor the way an overly protective mother shields her retarded child. Often one must look in the obscurity of the middle pages of the *Times* or the *P.-I.* to find out that something may be wrong in the city. Or, if one is curious enough to ask "someone who should know," the answer is usually that things are getting better, that you shouldn't believe the things you read in the newspapers.

Beneath it, though, the real sin of the city reveals itself. Seattle overextends time after time, and then tries to swallow its own waste. "These things ought not so to be." Optimism has to have some ground in reality. Saying that it's all right does not make it so.

What is needed in Seattle is genuine understanding of the wasted dreams and broken hearts of its citizens. An articulate, honest stand, stated in words that Leschi would understand. No more nonsense, no more pie-in-the-sky solutions, no more dependence on the benevolence of churches.

Seattle is terrified of admitting that it has made mistakes. Confront a prominent Seattleite with statistics that show trouble in the city and he will immediately go on the defensive, denying, questioning the validity of the figures, saying "Not so."

But it is so. And no justification any member of the establishment may offer could change it one iota. It's sad to say, but whenever someone states that Seattle's economy is coming back, one can only look at the history of the city and smile politely.

Ole and Dave

Ole Hanson took his oath of office as mayor of Seattle on March 5, 1918, and almost immediately began to butt his head and ego against labor. He was scared of the Chamber of Commerce when he took office, but he soon changed his mind when he got wind of the Red Menace lurking in the IWW. "I soon learned that overalls did not denote a greater degree of honesty than broadcloth." Ole says that he broke the General Strike of 1919, and, in so doing, the back of the Wobblie movement. He then set out to be President, leaving a very open door for the young laundry-truck driver Dave Beck.

Ole once said:

> Americanism should be a regular course in all schools, just the same as arithmetic and grammar. It is the very

warp and woof of our civilization. Surely it is important
—essential. I would rather have my children understand
the history and ideals of our country than that they learn
Latin or Greek. I contend that no unbiased, unpreju-
diced person can sincerely advocate the overthrow of this
Government if he understands just what kind of government it is. There are so many false teachers of soap-
bubble Utopias that it is well that, right at the start, the
children should be taught Americanism and also be
shown the fallacy and universal failure of the quack cure-
alls that are ever and anon offered to the gullible.

All Dave Beck talked about was his Teamsters Union
being part of a city of little millionaires. Beck went for the
long haul, not the short burst of ego-glory of Ole Hanson.
I don't think Ole was a liar; he honestly believed that his
putting down of a strike that never really had a chance, that
had, in fact, shut itself down, qualified him to run for
President, to be the leading anti-Bolshevik in America, to
put on an act that only Senator Joseph McCarthy, with the
aid of a nation newly attuned to television, could top.

Ole was just giddy. Puffed up with the fact that the first
general labor strike in America had taken place in the still
hick town of Seattle (it had been, after all, only some
twenty years after the Klondike gold strike put its name on
the map), and exhilarated with his illusion that he was the
one who stopped it.

Like many other Seattleites before him and after him, he
was no politician, just a little man from a little town with
dreams of gold dust clouding his eyes.

Beck was something different: a squat man with a big
powerful voice and a mind to go with it, he set about his
business with the sure hands of the laborer.

Ole Hanson wanted the world and all its treasures. He
wanted the whole United States to fall into his eager hands.

But, if it had, he wouldn't have known what to do with it.

He had his troubles with Leon Green, that mysterious Bolshevik whom everybody seemed to hate; but, then, Dave Beck had his troubles with Harry Bridges, that unmysterious Bolshevik whom nobody except longshoremen seemed to like.

The difference between Hanson and Beck is that one wanted to soar to Mount Olympus and the other joined the Elks Lodge.

To Hanson, the strike of 1919 became a religious crusade: it was not a labor problem; it was God versus the Devil, and being the mayor of Seattle meant that Ole Hanson was an Angel of the Lord, if not (and he surely would not have uttered this notion, no matter how much he may have entertained it) the Son Himself. I'm sure he envisioned candles flickering in churches at the very mention of the name Leon Green.

Dave Beck was first and last a capitalist. Driving his laundry truck taught him that there was no reason why people sitting on a seat with a wheel in front of them shouldn't get as much as those with pen and paper; it also taught him that it must be much more comfortable in the swivel chair than in the bouncing driver's seat. So Dave Beck bought, embraced, and made his own sweetbriar bride out of the Seattle Spirit. There was no love here, no David Denny romance, just recognition of what was. If the Chamber of Commerce once feared "Beck's goons," they began to revere the member of the Board of Regents of the University of Washington.

The red-faced, rough-handed millionaire made it big because he refused to allow Budweiser beer to cross the Cascades; and, because instead of talking to men like Harry Bridges, he talked to men like Henry Broderick. It all made sense. There was never any major problem between labor and management in Seattle, only money and, occasionally, race. The latter was impossible to resolve, but the former needed only the Elks Lodge.

The Elks is hardly the Pacific Club or the Athletic Club, but in the Northwest it's a starting place for a labor leader to make his name. No radical he; he's an Elk. And so it was to be for Dave Beck; knowing business, he became a businessman, and, remaining a labor man, he dragged labor, at least his Teamsters, along with him.

The Reds, particularly Harry Bridges, got in his way, and he could get rid of them by grabbing on to the coattails of the establishment and then telling them what he wanted. No Ole Hanson *vox populi;* just, do it my way and I'll do it yours. And no "please."

The establishment eventually bought it. They knew that Beck was on their side; he only wanted to make money, not trouble. So he was finally called upon to help organize Greater Seattle and nobly served the university, while crazy old Ole got humiliated and staggered off into the wilderness of his own broken ego.

Clarence Darrow summed up Ole pretty well:

> Is Ole Hanson hard to understand? Is he? Doesn't he show, all over him, the marks of a cheap poser? Doesn't he show all over him the evidence of a light-hearted notoriety hunter? Think of it, gentlemen! Imagine one of you. Suppose you had been the hero of this bloody strike. Suppose you had preserved civilization and Americanism because you were such a great and such a brave and such a noble Mayor? Suppose that you had bared your breast to this mob, that opens up milk stations and eating houses and carefully guards the peace of the city. Suppose that you had earned the plaudits of your fellow man and the encomiums of the press? Suppose that you had done that and suppose that you had been heralded by State's Attorneys the great savior of the world, what would you have done?

Well, I fancy you would have stuck to your job. I fancy you would have stayed right there and run the job. But not Ole, oh no, not Ole. When he was advertised from one end of America to another for his fool proclamation because he was the jumping jack Mayor of Seattle, when his advertising was worth thousands in lecture courses, he forthwith lays down his job and leaves Seattle to go to the dogs, or to the workingmen, as the case may be.

The captain deserts the army, and the pilot gets off the ship and lets Seattle go to the devil while he rakes in the shekels.

Now, that is Ole; that is Ole Hanson, the cheap vaudeville performer. . . .

Why, he said he needed the money.

That is a fine excuse for a patriot, and pretty near all of the professional patriots need the money; that is the reason they are professional patriots, they need the money.

Before the strike of the Newspaper Guild against the Seattle *Post-Intelligencer* in 1936, the establishment mistrusted Dave Beck. Every labor-management dispute was attributed directly to him, whether he was involved or not.

The strike changed all that. Although not nearly so dramatic as the General Strike that catapulted Ole Hanson to instant fame, it unearthed some strange bedfellows: Guild members, mostly orderly middle-class types who had been trying to organize the *P.-I.* so that they could get higher wages; "goons" from the waterfront, hired to add some muscle; Commonwealth Federation members, always ready for a cause; and every available Communist and radical in the area. The blame, of course, was tossed right at Dave Beck. He wasn't involved. What he did, with that remarkable cunning of his, was to go out and settle the strike.

What the establishment learned from that was what his own Teamsters had known all along, that Dave Beck couldn't stand Communists or radicals. He viewed labor as business, he had no banners to wave or flags to fly, save for the American flag. "Let's sit down over a cup of coffee and we can settle this thing," seems to have been his motto. All he wanted was a partnership for himself and his Teamsters in the American Dream, hand in hand with business.

This came as an incredible shock to the vested business-men. Here was a labor leader who didn't want their heads or their jobs, simply a separate but equal job of his own.

A difficult pill for Greed to swallow. Since its inception, the owners of Seattle had looked with a mixture of hatred and fear at the men who made their money for them, wor-ried that at any time they might rise up and overthrow them. And then along comes a man whom they've always abhorred settling a strike they couldn't handle and he only asks for $25,000.

But that's the kind of man Dave Beck was; to borrow a phrase from William Speidel, he was first and last a "Son of the Profits." Unlike Ole Hanson, who would turn crimson and scream at the sight of a Red flag, Dave Beck would sit back, think, and then calmly, carefully lower the flag. He was not about to make a fool of him-self.

By the time Beck made his presence public, the City of the Future was firmly implanted on Puget Sound, and it only needed a little improving. There were no Leon Greens for Dave Beck to fight, just some confused "native-born Americans" to persuade.

Dave Beck understood the Seattle Spirit and embraced it, made it his. Ole Hanson had it, forgot it, and left it completely at the first sniff of national recognition.

Two different Seattleites—Ole Hanson, bloated with a

flush of glory, thought the nation was his for the taking, while Dave Beck was able to bide his time and simply take his piece of the city.

Squatter's Rights

> They [the Indians] were squatters, what else? They had no title to the land.

> —Henry Broderick, nonagenarian Seattle
> realtor, in an interview in August, 1972

Chief Sealth, speaking at the signing of the Treaty of Port Elliott, January 22, 1855:

Yonder sky that has wept tears of compassion upon my people for centuries untold, and which to us appears changeless and eternal, may change. Today is fair. To-morrow it may be overcast with clouds. My words are like the stars that never change. Whatever Seattle says the great chief at Washington can rely upon with as much certainty as he can upon the return of the sun or the seasons. The White Chief says that Big Chief at Washington sends us greetings of friendship and good-will. This is kind of him for we know he has little need of our friendship in return. His people are many. They are like the grass that covers vast prairies. My people are few. They resemble the scattering trees of a storm-swept plain. The great, and I presume—good White Chief sends us word that he wishes to buy our lands but is willing to allow us enough to live comfortably. This indeed appears just, even generous, for the Red Man no longer has rights that he need respect, and the offer may be wise also, as we are no longer in need of an extensive country.

There was a time when our people covered the land as the waves of a wind-ruffled sea cover its shell-paved floor, but that time long since passed away with the greatness of tribes that are now but a mournful memory. I will not dwell on, nor mourn over, our untimely decay, nor reproach my paleface brothers with hastening it as we too may have been somewhat to blame.

Youth is impulsive. When our young men grow angry at some real or imaginary wrong, and disfigure their faces with black paint, it denotes that their hearts are black, and that they are often cruel and relentless, and our old men and old women are unable to restrain them. Thus it has ever been. Thus it was when the white men first began to push our forefathers further westward. But let us hope that the hostilities between us may never return. We would have everything to lose and nothing to gain. Revenge by young men is considered gain, even at the cost of their own lives, but old men who stay at home in times of war, and mothers who have sons to lose, know better.

Our good father at Washington—for I presume he is now our father as well as yours, since King George has moved his boundaries further north—our great and good father, I say, sends us word that if we do as he desires he will protect us. His brave warriors will be to us a bristling wall of strength, and his wonderful ships of war will fill our harbors so that our ancient enemies far to the northward—the Hydas and Tsimpsians, will cease to frighten our women, children and old men. Then in reality will he be our father and we his children. But can that ever be? Your God is not our God! Your God loves your people and hates mine. He folds his strong protecting arms lovingly about the pale face and leads him by the hand as a father leads his infant son—but He has forsaken His red children—if they are really his. Our God, the Great Spirit, seems also to have forsaken us. Your God made your people wax strong every day. Soon they will fill all the land. Our people are ebbing away like a rapidly receding tide that will never return. The white man's God cannot love our people or He would protect them. They seem to be orphans who can look nowhere for help. How then can we be brothers? How can your God become our God and renew our prosperity and awaken in us the dreams of returning greatness? If we have a common heavenly father He must be partial—for He came to His paleface children. We never saw him. He gave you laws but had no word for his red children whose teeming multitudes once filled this vast continent as stars fill the firmament. No; we are two distinct races with separate origins and separate destinies. There is little in common between us.

To us the ashes of our ancestors are sacred and their resting place is hallowed ground. You wander far from the graves of your ancestors and seemingly without regret. Your religion was written upon tablets of stone by the iron finger of your God so that you could not forget. The Red Man could never comprehend nor remember it. Our religion is the traditions of our ancestors—the dreams of our old men, given them in solemn hours of night by the Great Spirit; and the visions of our sachems, and is written in the hearts of our people.

Your dead cease to love you and the land of their nativity as soon as they pass the portals of the tomb and wander way beyond the stars. They are soon forgotten and never return. Our dead never forget the beautiful world that gave them being. They still love its verdant valleys, its murmuring rivers, its magnificent mountains, sequestered vales and verdant lined lakes and bays, and ever yearn in tender, fond affection over the lonely hearted living, and often return from the Happy Hunting Ground to visit, guide, console and comfort them.

Day and night cannot dwell together. The Red Man has ever fled the approach of the White Man, as the morning mist flees before the morning sun.

However, your proposition seems fair and I think that my people will accept it and will retire to the reservation you offer them. Then we will dwell apart in peace, for the words of the Great White Chief seem to be the words of nature speaking to my people out of dense darkness.

It matters little where we pass the remnant of our days. They will not be many. The Indians' night promises to be dark. Not a single star of hope hovers above his horizon. Sad-voiced winds moan in the distance. Grim fate seems to be on the Red Man's Trail, and wherever he goes he will hear the approaching footsteps of his fell destroyer and prepare stolidly to meet his doom, as does the wounded doe that hears the approaching footsteps of the hunter.

A few more moons. A few more winters—and not one of the descendants of the mighty hosts that once moved over this broad land or lived in happy homes, protected by the Great Spirit, will remain to mourn over the graves of a people—once more powerful and hopeful than yours. But why should I mourn at the untimely fate of my people? Tribe follows tribe, and nation follows nation, like the waves of the sea. It is the order of nature, and regret is useless. Your time of decay may be distant, but it will surely come, for even the White Man whose God walked and talked with him as friend with friend, cannot be exempt from the common destiny. We may be brothers, after all. We will see.

We will ponder your proposition and when we decide we will let you know. But should we accept it, I here and now make this condition that we will not be denied the privilege without molestation of visiting at any time the tombs of our ancestors, friends and children. Every part of this soil is sacred in the estimation of my people. Every hillside, every valley, every plain and grove, has been hallowed by some sad or happy event in days long vanished. Even the rocks, which seem to be dumb and dead as they swelter in the sun along the silent shore, thrill with memories of stirring events connected with the lives of my people, and the very dust upon which you now stand responds more lovingly to their footsteps than to yours, because it is rich with the blood of our ancestors and our bare feet are conscious of the sympathetic touch. Our departed braves, fond mothers, glad, happy-hearted maidens, and even the little children who lived here and rejoiced here for a brief season, will love these somber solitudes and at eventide they greet shadowy returning spirits. And when the last Red Man shall have perished, and the memory of my tribe shall have become a myth among the White Men, these shores will swarm with the invisible dead of my tribe, and when your children's children think themselves alone in the field, the store, the shop, upon the highway, or in the silence of the pathless woods, they will not be alone. In all the earth there is no place dedicated to solitude. At night when the streets of your cities and villages are silent and you think them deserted, they will throng with the returning hosts that once filled them and still love this beautiful land. The White Man will never be alone.

Let him be just and deal kindly with my people, for the dead are not powerless. Dead, did I say? There is no death, only a change of worlds.

The Indians of the Pacific Northwest had what was to the white man a totally incomprehensible notion of their relationship to the land and to the salmon, which was their principal sustenance. They thought of the land as their mother and the salmon as their brother. They ate it, but when it passed through their systems, it was reborn, to return in the next salmon run. Just as Chief Sealth said, ". . . no death, only a change of worlds." It was the sort of harmony that Henry David Thoreau, like a squat Diogenes, dedicated his life to finding. It was no accident that his last words were "Moose. Indian," with no explanation given and none needed. Maybe if Thoreau, rather than Governor Stevens, had negotiated the treaties things would have been different. But probably not.

The Indians simply weren't fit enough, particularly those tribes of the lower Puget Sound area. When Arthur Denny set his sights on the land he wanted for his city, it was already inhabited, but by some crazy simian creature unfit to dwell with civilized man. The Muckleshoots, Puyallups, and Nisquallis could not understand or abide by the white man's laws or notions of his superiority. To the Indians a man was not what he did but what he *was;* the fact of existence alone was enough to bring honor to life and to death. So very pure, so very Greek, so very Indian that it is no wonder white men could not understand it.

Doing was what life was all about to the white man, not just being. Notions of living in some sort of concert with nature were poppycock. You go and take something and make it yours and hold on to it. Then expand and get more. Imagine thinking that a fish you ate and then excreted would come back the next season!

You eat because you're hungry, because you've worked hard and you've got to work again. But the Indians made something religious out of it, and not just a "thank you, God," sitting down to table. A real ceremony.

There are tired old men who still tell stories of the glories their grandfathers found on Elliott Bay, but they aren't Indians. Indians are now trying to deal with the present, as they've always done, as well as the past. They want their

fish back, and King County of the State of Washington gave
them two moonlight outings, July 15 and 16, in the year of
Our Lord 1973, to catch their load in Lake Washington, and
then back it went to the sport fishermen.

In the summer of 1972, Lake Washington was a battle-
ground that would have warmed the cockles of any
pioneer's heart. In the early hours of Tuesday morning,
July 18, three Muckleshoots were arrested after catching
sixty sockeye salmon in a 200-foot gill net. That was just the
beginning.

Don Hannula, bylining in the Seattle *Times* of Thursday,
July 20, said:

> In the still of last night the state stalked Indians on
> Lake Washington while the Indians stalked the sockeye
> salmon.
>
> The Indians say they caught 105 sockeye.
>
> The state didn't catch any Indians.
>
> . . . W. S. Miller, Fisheries Department enforcement
> officer, said three state boats were patrolling the lake last
> night.
>
> He said enforcement officers saw "about 15 to 20" Indi-
> ans gathered at Rainier Beach about 10:30 P.M. He said
> three of them went out in a boat and returned about 12:30
> A.M., then loaded their skiff on a truck and left. He said
> a youth held up two sockeye.
>
> Miller said he "couldn't tell for sure" in the dark if the
> Indians had put a net in the lake.
>
> He said no arrests were made because "it didn't look
> like they were doing any serious fishing." He said when
> the youth held up the two sockeye "it looked like a
> setup." Miller said enforcement officials couldn't tell if
> the Indians caught the two sockeye or brought them to
> the lake in an attempt to get arrested.
>
> Miller said he thought the fishermen were Muckle-
> shoots.

Charles Willoghby, Kent, chairman of the Snoqualmie Indian Fishermen, acknowledged that a youth held up two sockeye, but said the state didn't see 103 more left in the boat. Willoghby said a 100-foot net was used. The Indians hoisted boat, net and salmon on the truck and the enforcement men didn't move in for a closer look. There were fifty Indians on shore, Willoghby said.

Willoghby said the Snoqualmies, who also claim a special treaty right to fish the off-reservation waters that were accustomed grounds of their ancestors, have no quarrel with the Muckleshoots.

"Last year the state made us fish under the Muckleshoots' agreement," Willoghby said. "We want to fish as Snoqualmies this year."

Pretty dry and formal in the reporting, but what a great, ironic, humor-filled move.

No wonder the "sport fishermen" got red in the neck.

But when else are Indians going to fish, except at night? Off the reservations, they are at the white man's mercy, captives of his kindness.

Up until a very short time ago, it was a virtual impossibility for a northwest Indian to get a job off the reservation. There was gandy-dancing on the railroads, until automation took those jobs away, and there was berry-picking. Aside from those, nothing. Now, thanks to people like Elizabeth Morris and the Indian Center in Seattle, things are slowly changing. The Indian Center houses programs such as Talent Search; an education program; an ex-offender program, which helps prepare parole plans; the Legal Assistance Program; the Youth Recreation Program; Employment Assistance; and the Technical Assistance Program.

Elizabeth Morris:　————————

My attitude on poverty is that we have a right to poverty if we want it; but we want to be left alone to our poverty. We don't want to have to live in a frame house. If we happen to like a log cabin and to hunt and to fish, we should be permitted to do that. My attitude about reservations is that it is all that is left of our land. And I like it. I don't want to end the reservations. I would like to improve the conditions for the people that are there. But some kinds of improvement we don't want. We don't want money just for money's sake. We don't want a bank account and all of that kind of jazz. We would like to have enough money to be able to feed and clothe our children and enough to get by with. Another thing about attitudes, Indians don't want to save up money to build fences around places. You know, you say that Henry Broderick said that we were squatters. Well, who made the titles? We didn't even know how to read or write.

Q.: Would the Indians like to have the kind of life that they traditionally had before the white man came?

E.M.: We can never have it again. It is just gone. I mean we can do certain parts of it, but it is just now impractical. What we are trying to do now is to retain what little we have left of our culture, but at the same time we are trying to be bicultural. We have to be.

Q.: You mean you want to become industrialized?

E.M.: Well, not completely. There is some of it that we will always reject, but we want our people to be able to make it either on the reservation or here. We want them to be Indian enough and live like that if they want to; and at the same time, if they come into the city, we want them to be able to compete for jobs.

Whenever Indians, or whenever any people are permitted to do their own thing, in their own way, they'll make it. It's when you try to get in and make them do it your way that it is wrong, because your way isn't always right for another person. And this is what this greater society has tried to do to all minorities. We have always had to fit into your slots.

Q.: And the fact that you did not fit into them correctly was taken as a sign of your inferiority?

E.M.: Yes, and you weren't bright because you couldn't make it in their schools. But when it's done with our own people who have already been through all of this mess, they are able to explain to the students in a meaningful way: I know what you are going through. And this is the way to handle it. Because by the time you have been through it all and made it, you know how to make it.

The idea behind such places as the Indian Center is not to take the Indian out of the Indian, so that he could try to pass in the white man's community, but rather to give him a sense of racial and cultural integrity—pride in the very thing the white man had taught and forced him to be ashamed of: his Indianness.

It's no easy job. A century of brainwashing can wreak incredible havoc on the human spirit, and, in spite of the teachings of our forefathers, the Indians *are* human beings.

Leschi was chief of the Nisquallis. A park in Seattle is named after him now, but in his prime he was strung up in the purest sense of the pioneer necktie party.

According to most accounts of the period, Leschi was an intelligent, sensitive, and very proud leader of his people.

So proud, in fact, that he refused to accept the white man's verdict.

On December 26, 1854, the Treaty of Medicine Creek between the Nisquallis and Puyallups and the United States government was, supposedly, signed. The treaty raised more problems than it solved.

First was the problem of language. The negotiations were conducted in the Chinook jargon, a strange admixture of Indian, French, and English, barely usable for bartering purposes and totally unsuitable to any kind of diplomatic subtleties. As Owen Bush of Governor Stevens's staff said (quoted by Ezra Meeker in his book *Pioneer Reminiscences*):

> I could talk the Indian languages, but Stevens did not seem to want anyone to interpret in their own tongue, and had that done in Chinook. Of course, it was utterly impossible to explain the treaties to them in Chinook. Stevens wanted me to go into the war [which followed the treaty-signing], but I wouldn't do it. I know it was his bad management that brought on the war, and I wouldn't raise a gun against those people [Nisquallis] who had always been so kind to us when we were weak and needy.

It was a treaty delivered in infantile language to the leaders of a people who were being treated as uncomprehending animals, by a man (Stevens) who, at least according to Meeker, was drunk at the time. No wonder Leschi got mad.

Further: under the terms of the treaty the Indians gave the white government 2,240,000 acres of land in exchange for $32,500 (to be paid over a twenty-year period) and three reservations of 1,280 acres each, which could be cut in size according to future governmental decisions.

And there was the fishing clause: Article III.

The right of taking fish at all usual and accustomed grounds and stations is further secured to said Indians in common with all citizens of the Territory, and of erecting temporary houses for the purpose of curing, together with the privilege of hunting, gathering roots and berries, and pasturing their horses on open and unclaimed lands: Provided, however, That they shall not take shell fish from any beds staked or cultivated by citizens, and that they shall alter all stallions not intended for breeding horses and shall keep up and confine the latter.

Privilege.

Leschi was there at the time and denied that he signed the treaty, which gave his tribe an unfarmable, arid plain far away from the fish; he claimed his signature was forged and set about more important business: saving the dignity of his people.

That meant war.

Leschi didn't really want it, probably no more than Chief Sealth did when he signed virtually the same treaty at Point Elliott a month later. But Leschi could not accept the white man's terms. American whites, called the Bostons by the Indians, were a different breed from the Hudson's Bay Company of the English. The King George men, as the Indians called them, wanted trade; the Bostons wanted the Indians' land. Too much for Leschi. He went out and preached the gospel of eternal damnation for the Indians unless they killed the whites before they were overwhelmed by them.

He was too late with too little. The gunboat *Decatur* was anchored in Seattle's harbor when Leschi and his Nisquallis came over the hills on January 26, 1855, and the big (to them) guns drove them off. This stamped Leschi as a "bad Indian," one who had to be caught and killed. In the fall of

1856 he was captured, brought to trial, and after one hung jury hanged on February 19, 1858. He was convicted of killing a white man at the outset of the fighting. And—in spite of pleading on the parts of white and red alike (including old Chief Sealth, the white man's friend) that what he did, if he did it, was an act of war—his execution was that of a common murderer.

In guilty return, his name was stuck on a park in front of which condominiums grow like cancer cells and "sport" fisherman shoo Indians away as though they were flies.

But the spirit of Leschi remains powerful because he was proud of his people and the land they lived with. And that spirit, completely without the market capabilities of the Seattle Spirit, bites hard at the gut.

Today the Indians of western Washington are much better organized than they were in Leschi's time. There is less reliance on one-man leadership; in fact, many Indians look back with outright scorn at men like Chief Sealth and others like him who made deals with the white man. And there is much less bickering between tribes. They have come to realize that theirs is a common cause, and despite the good intentions of many liberal whites, it is a problem they alone must deal with.

The "uncommon controversy" (to borrow a title from a truly marvelous book) over fishing rights and the consequent fish-ins of recent years is as vitally symbolic as it is real. The Indians want and need the fish, but their words and actions are also telling the white man that they now can read and speak his language and he can no longer, like Governor Stevens, hold the billy club of the Chinook jargon over their heads.

They want their own education, not what the white man deems proper for them. They want to handle their own affairs, not have some bureau in Washington take care of problems. The Great White Father is dead and gone, God rest his soul. And they want—particularly the Indians on the Olympic Peninsula—their reservations *clean:* if the white man comes onto their land, he damn well better pick up his trash.

Quite a difference from the way things used to be. As short a time as ten years ago, I went to La Push and there, facing the beautiful Pacific, were twenty-five to thirty broken-down cars, a coast guard station, and a closed "laundromat" (a shack housing three rusty and battered washing machines).

Henry Broderick had his ideas as to the blame for those conditions.

> Q.: What kind of responsibilities do you think we owe the Indians now? Anything in terms of compensation?
>
> H.B.: Don't you think we have done something for the Indians? We created all of these reservations and they half ruined them because they were on the reservation and they didn't have to work and they all got lazy.
>
> Q.: Lazy, but there was nothing to work for.
>
> H.B.: See, you can't afford to do too much for anybody unless they work for it. The Indian is a great example. It made a loafer out of him.

No more.

Now the red man demands his rights. Not only fish, but his dignity as a human being. He knows that the white man is not about to offer him that, so he will just take it using the white man's words and tactics. Play upon his anger for a while. Use his agencies, his courts, his media. Facing the gun of planned extinction, there is no recourse. Nonviolent (unlike unfortunate, dignified Leschi), the Indians face "the Man" arms akimbo, saying: "This is the way you want it."

The Indians want their squatter's rights.

And the Indian Center has now moved to larger quarters in the old Henry Broderick Building in downtown Seattle.

Race Relations

I'm a capitalist and imperialist dog who loves money and works hard for it, and I don't think I should give it away to anybody else, I think everybody should get what they work for. So that's me and I still work for it and I don't think I should give it away or divide it if I work for it.

I'm in the same boat with Henry Broderick and William Allen of Boeing and all the rest of the captains. I'm a Black capitalist and I feel the same as they feel. I started off with a little money working and I worked for mine.

—Fitzgerald Beaver, editor of *The Facts,* the Northwest's largest black-owned publication

Seattle is not overtly a racist city. Minority groups have at times been useful, in fact necessary, to her economy, but when those times pass, true Seattleites would like the foreigners and those of different skin colors just to disappear.

The Puritans had it easy—they had a whole continent to force the Indians into, away from the lands they wanted for themselves. But the Denny party could only force them into the sea, something no humane person could do. The Puget Sound Indians taught the white man how to fish, pick berries, build and paddle canoes, but after that, except for a brief period of illicit glory at Pennell's Illahee, they had nothing profitable to offer. They were rewarded for their labors with the only thing the "owners" of the land had to offer: reservations and fishing rights, given to them in terms (except for guns) that they could barely understand. The white man made some mistakes, like giving the Indians the Olympic Peninsula (something he's tried for more than a century, with little success, to rectify), but on the whole things worked out well and the Indians (with the exception of Leschi's brief rebellion) were put away quite peacefully.

In the early days of Seattle there were also bad whites to deal with. The Swedes, Germans, and Norwegians who had been driven West, not out of ambition but because of fear for their very existence, came to the Sound since they knew how to cut down trees. They smelled bad and spoke bad English; all they did well was wield an axe. But who —particularly those of the Denny party—wants an axe-wielder for a neighbor? Again the problem of hired help. Bring in those you don't want, and they want to stay. Some of the white laborers managed to assimilate: learning the language and putting down their axes, they found that money was to be made by wearing a suit and looking dour. Others, the really dumb ones, stayed up in the woods getting more and more angry, until finally they became the feared desperadoes of the Sound area—the Wobblies of the IWW. Coming down from the woods on a Saturday night was no longer a joke.

But even if they had Red Communist hearts, their faces were still white. The police could deal with them. In virgin Seattle, the "yumping yimminey" foreigner could be put in his place.

Not so the pigtailed foreigner, with his funny eyes and obsequious manner, carrying a satchel-bag. *There* was a threat. Or, rather, the strangeness of the Chinese *became* a threat. In *Skid Road*, Murray Morgan describes what happened:

> The Chinese had been popular once. They had been imported in large numbers by the railroad builders when

cheap labor was needed. When the Chinese arrived, the Western people had looked on them as genii who would bring from the East on their narrow backs the much desired tracks. The Chinese, one and all, were called "John," and the stories of John's prowess as a construction worker almost reached the status of folk legend. John could work twelve hours on a handful of rice; impassive John could handle blasting jobs that other men were too nervous to carry out; brave John would work all day at the end of a hundred-foot rope, chiseling notches for trestle supports; inscrutable John had the best poker-face in a poker-loving nation. Good old John.

And then the final sections of track were laid, the golden spikes were driven, and the construction workers poured into the western cities, into Tacoma and Portland, San Francisco and Seattle. The streets teemed with restless men, men with money to burn; restless men, soon broke, the Chinese among them. The fact that the Chinese were accustomed to receiving less than the white men no longer seemed laughable to the white workers; with the construction boom over and business slow, there was competition for every job—and fear of economic competition always increases prejudice. The hard-working, industrious Chinese who were willing to take any job, to accept any wage, became symbols of discontent to the unemployed. "Go Home, John," the slogans said, "Go, John."

Lots of them wanted to go. So many that the ships were glutted. They knew they weren't wanted, particularly with shotguns at their backs.

Seattle needed to get rid of the Chinese, and it was no mere labor problem. Their skin did them in. If the grime of the unrepentant logger or the gibbering redness of the Indian were not welcome in respectable Seattle, how could it countenance yellow faces? So Seattle shipped the Chinese down to the boats with quietude and alacrity, until the boats started swaying with overload and some Chinese had to remain ashore and open laundries and restaurants and the little gambling joints that my grandfather was so addicted to. After the exodus, those who remained were known for their sins. Every one of them *had* to be addicted to opium—it made no difference whether they had even heard the word or not, they used it; you could tell by the color of their skin that they used it, and for some unexplained reason, it made them wily.

Wily, dumb, smelly, and lazy are great words to use to describe the unwanted. In 1886 the Seattle *Call* (the self-proclaimed voice of labor) described the Chinese for its readers: "the two-bit conscience of the scurvy opium fiend . . . the treacherous almond-eyed sons of Confucius . . . chattering, round-mouthed lepers . . . these yellow rascals who have infected our Western country, the rat-eating Chinamen."

On February 7, 1886, after organizations had been formed, meetings held, and speeches given, a startling thing happened. To quote Murray Morgan once again:

> Shortly after seven o'clock the mob moved into the Chinese district. The Sinophobes were organized in groups of five: "order committees," they called themselves. The leader of a committee would pound upon the door of a Chinese house and say they had come to see if the city health regulations were being obeyed. Once inside, the leader would inform the Chinese that the building was condemned as a hazard to health and warn them that if they wished to avoid serious trouble they would get out of town at once. The steamer *Queen of the Pacific* was at the ocean dock, about to sail for San Francisco. Did they want to leave with her? The Chinese had no choice. With their doors open and hundreds of determined workingmen milling in the street outside, they could only say yes. Once the Chinese had agreed to go,

the chairman would tell the people waiting outside to "help out the heathens." The mob would rush in, carry out all the household goods and pile them in wagons, and hustle the Chinese off to the ocean dock.

They couldn't get them all onto the boat, not that day or any other. People died; others were brought to trial; still others survived in the backwash of hatred.

I first met a Japanese when I was in the eighth grade. She and I became friends, and one time I asked her what her parents did. She told me that before the war her father had been a gardener, that during the war they had been in camp, and, since then, he'd had trouble getting a job. I remember feeling sorry about the job trouble, but also feeling envious of her going to camp for such a long time.

I asked my mother about it and she told me that the Japanese had to be kept in camps during the war. I asked why and she answered that it was for their own protection, because we were at war with them. I couldn't figure out why anybody would want to be at war with Gail.

What is the difference between the mob cries of "John, go home" herding the Chinese to the docks in 1886, and the leer on the face of G. S. Hanff, barber in Kent, Washington, as he was photographed in 1942, pointing proudly to a sign that reads: WE DON'T WANT ANY JAPS BACK HERE—EVER!"?

Scruffy little Kent, with its funny car shows and its dependence on the deranged bettors from Seattle, doesn't want Japs to this day. Porn stars or failed Vegas lounge acts, yes, but Japs, no—nor Chinks, nor Niggers, nor Indians, just a gaggle of white trash from the fringes of Seattle.

But "white trash" are trash only because of their manners, occupation, or habits and thereby unsuitable to live in respectable neighborhoods. They are, however, still considered to be white men. With yellow, red, and black it is a totally different story.

After the abortive Indian War, the Indians went reluctantly to their reservations. After the Chinese were shipped out, those who remained tried to disappear into a proud obscurity. After the Everett and Centralia massacres, the Wobblies hightailed it back into the woods. Each group tried to hide from the oppressors, the "owners" of the land.

But the biggest racial coup came on February 19, 1942, when President Roosevelt signed Executive Order 9066, removing 110,000 Japanese-Americans from their jobs and homes and placing them in camps. It was the largest single act of racism in American history. Hiding under the guise of national security and personal protection for those interred, it cut open America's festering wound once and for all, and true American fear, racial hatred, and jealousy were given a legal tool to accomplish effectively what they had wanted to do all along. We could get all the Japs at once, without any pretense at negotiation.

Listen to George Tokuda, a Japanese pharmacist:

My father was about nineteen or twenty when he first came to Seattle in 1905. He was a chauffeur here for a while, but then he ended up in Mukilteo. My mother left her baby, my older brother, in Japan, and followed; I was born in Mukilteo in 1912, and my brother joined us when I was seven and he was thirteen. I went to grade school in Mukilteo and to high school in Everett, and then took a course for four years in electrical trades. At that time I understood that the course was one of the best on the coast, and that if you got a B average or better for four years, you would be issued a Smith Institute certificate for the trade. Out of twenty-eight of us, six of us got it. All the other five had jobs waiting for them, but no matter how many times I went it was the same answer: no opening—if we hear of any, we'll let you know.

So that's when I went to the principal in Muk-ilteo, Mr. Black, to see what he thought, and it was he who told me that the reason I was not getting work was because, let's face it, you know, because I was Japanese.

My father was working as a foreman of a brewery then, and I decided I had better go to the university, but I didn't have the prerequisite high school courses I needed to get in, which were at least two years of a foreign language and a year of chemistry. So I asked Mrs. McGee, who was teaching junior high school, to tutor me in Latin and I had to go after school, starting in January, and then study chem. at Everett High. They let me finish chem. 2 without any lab work even because they knew I was good, and that's how I got into the university. I think I owe that to Mr. Black because he made me face what I was up against in the trades, and he said to take some course over at the university which I could use either to go into business for myself, or work for someone.

. . . When I got out of school in 1932 I worked for a Japanese man who had a drugstore, for two years, and I wasn't happy there, so I got a job at Bartell for about nine months at $9 per week as a stock boy. I wasn't happy there either. At the end of six months when I asked for a raise they said, okay, we'll give you a raise, and transferred me to another store, where they had fired the janitor. They made me do the work of the janitor, plus the work of stock boy, which I did for two days. . . .

Then I heard of this job where a lady was looking for someone to work in her drugstore because her husband, a pharmacist, had died. I worked very hard there and she was so happy with it that before the year was up she had offered to sell the store to me. She treated me like her own son, really, and in 1935 I took over the store. I paid $500 down, and $20 a month, I think it cost $2,900 in all, and by the time of the evacuation, I had built it up to the point where we had about $15,000 in stock. Then war came in '41, after Pearl Harbor, and by that time I had two stores. I had opened a branch on 12th Avenue.

Then we got stuck into camp, first at Puyallup at the fair grounds for three months in the hot summer, and then we got transferred to the permanent camp in Idaho. That's when I asked if I could be released for a few days to come to Seattle so I could take care of my affairs. They said no, and sold both my stores for $1,900—stock, fixtures, and all. They must have been worth, easy, $26,000 or $28,000; I had at least $5,000 worth of stock in the 12th Avenue store, and with the main store stock on 18th and Yesler, it was worth $20,000 in just stock alone. I did keep the fixtures from the 12th Avenue store—that's the only thing I have left.

I wasn't the only one—all of us on the West Coast. I remember I had a brand-new Chevy, I think I only had it for about a few months, and had just paid the down payment, and that went too. Everybody was coming to buy everything up for about ten cents on the dollar, so I sold it for almost nothing before I went to camp, because I had to get rid of it. A lot of us thought we were never coming back anyway. We weren't rational anymore, really. I asked one woman I had known quite well to run the store for me until I heard from the government

about what they could do for me in terms of a settlement, and she ran it for three months before it was
sold. I still remember when she came to Puyallup,
when I was still in there, at the end of the three-
month period, with about eighteen dollars in cash,
when here, you see, she was doing over a hundred
dollars a day. All my stocks were getting depleted;
you can't tell me she only had eighteen dollars left.

I was in camp in Idaho by fall of '42, and stayed
until about May of '43; that's when the government
slowly started to release those people that they felt
could make their way. Everyone west of Spokane,
whether they were citizens or had been born here
or not, if they were Japanese they had been put in
a camp. Army personnel came to the camp to recruit us to join the army, but that was one of the
reasons I wouldn't volunteer. Some of my best
friends did, but the way I felt, they had nothing to
lose, they were young, whereas I had lost two
stores, even my personal belongings that I had left
with people, most of which I never got back. They
didn't think we were ever coming back, they used
one excuse or another, but they didn't expect us to
come back for our things. . . .

We had to have two hundred dollars in our
pocket to show to them in order to get out, two
hundred dollars to prove to them, you know. So I
got out, and I ended up in Chicago, and the drugstore business there was no good—well, I didn't
think I could make a living working in one of the
chain stores at that time because, if I remember
correctly, the first job I was offered there in a drugstore was for thirty-five dollars a week. I almost
ended up taking care of pigs when the job was of-

fered to me, me and another druggist who had come to Chicago with me.

But we had another job offer aside from the pig farm, and that was as chemists for the Pabst brewery, so one day we packed and went to Milwaukee. All Japanese of military age at that time were classified as 4-C, and the 4-C classification meant aliens or those unfit for the U.S. Army, and it covered lots of different categories. So when we went to work for the brewery, we were thought of as more or less permanent employees because they had lost a lot of their young workers to the army and that is why, upon learning we were 4-C, they had phoned all the way from Milwaukee to Chicago so they could get druggists who wouldn't be taken for the military. When we got there, however, they saw we were "undesirable" for the U.S. Army, and that was it. We didn't get the jobs after all, so we had taken a trip from Chicago to Milwaukee for nothing.

We came back to Chicago and got jobs working in a sheet metal shop, working there about three months. Neither of us had ever done that kind of hard work before, and you should have seen us—I don't know how many boxes of Band-Aids we used up. Then we saw some young kids who were welding, and getting paid more than us. We started practicing welding right there on the job and in two weeks we had mastered the fundamentals of it. We quit and got a job as welders in another shop. For two and a half years we welded.

At one stage, oh about six months or so before we quit, I got my draft notice from Seattle, so I got on the train and came back to camp to enlist. My wife was in camp, she had gotten ill in Chicago and I couldn't take care of her because I was working, and she had come back to camp because her parents were there and my parents were there, and she had her baby there. When I was on the train, going back to enlist, I think it was North Platte where I got a newspaper and read that any man over the age of thirty-two they weren't taking, and I was over thirty-two. So I figure I might as well go back to the camp anyway, to visit my wife. My first-born, the baby who was born in the camp, is a retarded boy, and I believe it's because when my wife first got sick in Chicago, with kidney trouble, we had gone to a quack doctor who had treated her without knowing she was pregnant, which we didn't know either at the time. . . .

Before I had left Chicago, I had begun getting letters from the first Japanese to be repatriated and who were living in our old neighborhood again. They wrote me that the fellow, a Caucasian, who had bought my store, wouldn't sell to any Japanese, saying he didn't want Japs in his store. I don't think anyone in his right mind, operating a store in the international area of Seattle, could do something like that—unless he was crazy. Anyway, I got these letters asking me to come back to Seattle again for good and they would stand behind me one hundred percent.

So I came back to Seattle, in the fall of '45, and I couldn't wait to get back. I guess I'm just a country boy at heart—I had even forfeited my wages for my last week in Chicago because I wanted to get out of there so badly. . . .

About two months after I got back, I opened up a small cubbyhole drugstore, almost kitty-corner from where my store used to be. Three years later, the owner of my original store approached me—it had changed hands a number of times and he was the third owner to have it—and that's how I got back to the old corner on 18th and Yesler. That was in 1948, and we started getting back on our feet; the old customers came back.

When I had first opened the store in '35 the area there had been mainly Jewish; when I left it was about 50 percent Orientals, and quite a cosmopolitan area; when we came back in '46 it was 90 percent black. As years went by, the Orientals started coming back and re-establishing themselves in the old area, and times were very good to us then all through the fifties.

Then in '69 black riots started in Seattle, and I think we were the first store hit. Earlier in the year, I had been robbed at gunpoint, twice, and broken into many times before that, starting in about '65. . . . The neighborhood had become very rough and was getting worse as years went by, but we stayed. I had three fires within six months in 1969, and we couldn't stand it anymore, finally. So I closed down what little was left of the store and we went to Japan for a while, to get away from what we had been living through those past three years. . . .

After we got back from Japan, I moved the store four blocks away to this place here. We had to borrow to do it. I had no savings left, and only a third of the stock was salvageable from the other store.

Q.: Do you have any other children besides your first son?

G.T.: I have five altogether. One son is getting his masters in sociology at the University of Washington, a daughter has just graduated from the university in political science, and one daughter who has transferred from San Diego and will be entering the U as a sophomore. My oldest daughter is married and lives in Renton. She has her own home there.

Q.: How do they feel about all that's happened to their parents—do they feel a sense of bitterness about America?

G.T.: I have always told them about prejudice, and that being Japanese you have to expect a certain amount of it, there's no getting away from it, whether you were born here or not. Fortunately, in their grade school experiences here, they didn't experience prejudice. . . .

About twenty thousand Japanese people live in Seattle now. Before the war, about six thousand—and a lot of them didn't come back. But many young Japanese workers came from other parts of the country to work for Boeing during the big years.

Q.: How was the prejudice immediately after the war, then?

G.T.: When we first came back, we didn't know what to expect, which is why the Japanese wanted to return to the same area they had lived in before, which was among other things an Oriental neighborhood. I remember distinctly a couple of times when I went fishing, people would yell, hey Jap, get out of the bay, go fish somewhere else!

But getting back to my children. My daughter who's in political science, she's interested very much in minority problems, and she's working for the state now in a minority program. She says that after a couple of years, if she likes it, she'll go back and take law. I was almost afraid she was going to become an *activist*, because she originally had a scholarship to Whitman, one of the better colleges around here, and she went there her first year—in fact, she made the President's List first semester. She went to a restaurant in Walla Walla, where the school is located, sat down, and she sees all these people who came in after her being served before her. She came home and told me she just about stood up and screamed because she knew why. That is when prejudice became a personal experience for her, instead of something other people only told her about. She came back to Seattle, and enrolled in the U after that. . . .

Q.: Do you feel optimistic about Seattle's future?

G.T.: From what I see in cities back East, where there are such large minorities, especially blacks, integration there is really unheard of—I mean there's such a division between them and the white population. But here, there's a better chance of assimilation and integration than anywhere else I've seen.

Q.: Are the Japanese well integrated?

G.T.: Yes, after the war they were scattered around the city, more scattered at least than before the war when they all lived in the international district. And before the war, the Japanese here, their parents not having grown up or been educated in America, they still stuck to the old ways, the old culture. . . .

I think Seattle has a good future—if everyone stays rational and doesn't panic if a minority family moves in and suddenly everyone puts their house up for sale. I hope my kids won't have to go through what I did, or move way out into the suburbs to get away from all this. Crime has really become a problem all over the city. The police say they've turned the tide, but that's a biased opinion I would say, to some extent.

Another thing that's interesting. After I first moved into my new store here, a series of muggings and robberies started happening. It was so bad that I even went and called the police department and talked to the councilman who was in charge of street crime, and they said I should compile some statistics on what was happening, so I did. Sixty-eight people got mugged or robbed within a four-block radius of my store, and more than half of the victims were my customers who had come from the store, in broad daylight. And those sixty-eight were only ones I knew of *directly*, but there were plenty of others. This was in 1970.

Anyhow, the Japanese-American Citizens League had invited the police to come and talk to them about what could be done—people couldn't even walk outside, so I started closing up by six. Most of it was being done by black teenage kids. Some people I know were hit three or four times, and every single one of those sixty-eight were Japanese! I was invited to sit in and listen too when the police came to speak, and they said, you people are getting some of the best protection in the city—I still remember getting up and questioning them about that.

But I think what broke the back of crime in this area, the central area, is that many of those teenagers went on to more serious crimes and are in jail now, at least the ringleaders are. A number of Japanese have begun moving back into this area now, because they remember when they used to live here before the war. Japanese, the older ones, come from a culture where neighborhood ties are very important. When I was a boy, whole clans would work one sawmill or another, and the houses they lived in, all huddled together, were called Jap Town. It's like the Italians.

Q.: Do your children speak Japanese?

G.T.: My wife and I do, because we were exposed to it from our parents, but we speak English at home, and so do the kids.

Q.: Do they have much identification with Japanese culture?

G.T.: Sad to say, no. They are American. Much as we parents would like to see them marry their own kind, I wouldn't be surprised if they married Caucasians, because that's all they go around with. It's the times, and we can't change them back. One year, I couldn't believe it, but there were more Chinese-Japanese marriages around here than any other kind, and you know, historically they are the bitterest of enemies.

There's one last thing I'd like to go back and mention. When I went to grade school, I was the first Japanese student in Mukilteo, and Mukilteo was a very small town at that time. Since we Japanese lived in Jap Town, my father had the foresight to look ahead, and as soon as I was able to walk he sent me to a Caucasian nun, a French nun, Santé, so that I could go over and visit her and learn English. I had breakfast with her every morning. To this day I still remember her, and she was my introduction to Caucasian people. The other kids in Jap Town were surprised that there *were* Caucasians. When people passed our compound or traveling salesmen came to see us, the only way they addressed us was: Tokyo or Nippon.

Q.: You really were in camp twice, first in Jap Town, then the camp in Idaho. Minidoka.

G.T.: Yes. Minidoka will go down in history.

As Mr. Tokuda points out, hatred of the Japanese did not occur just in Seattle; the flames burned up and down the West Coast and the embers blew across the entire nation. All of a sudden there were no more Japs. And when they left for their camps, good American hands could clap with glee. In a quick orderly outburst, at least one group of the unwanted were disposed of.

It tore families apart: pitting Issei fathers against Nisei sons in the most unnatural manner imaginable. Native-born Japanese-Americans could fight for their country; their immigrant fathers could not. And even in this license there was hypocrisy. They were not allowed to fight in Asia, because in spite of their American birth there was the overwhelming fear they might be traitors. They were allowed to fight Italians in order to prove their devotion to their native America.

When the war ended, the hatred did not. Those who chose to return to their homes and businesses found them gone. They had to start from scratch. There were attempts made at reparation. But in such small, igno-minious sums as to be almost laughable. Anyway, how can the dignity and pride of a man be restored to him for $2,500? Yet many did return, to suffer in isolation. Not only were they hated by the whites, but by the Chinese as well, and not so much because Japan took China, but because many Chinese were forced to flee their homes during the evacuation for the simple reason that white eyes could not tell the difference between the Chinese and Japanese and this confusion was a good rea-son to get rid of the Chinese as well.

Although I was too young to understand, my relatives

remember the insanity of Seattle after the war. It is now viewed by many Seattleites through a haze of nostalgia. But when the Japanese returned, it was ugly: unveiled threats, no one to speak with, no place to live. Racial hatred never dies, but in Seattle it barely seems to hibernate. It is, and has been from the beginning, smoldering just under the surface, ready to explode at any opportunity.

Old Chief Sealth figured out the rules pretty quickly and did all he could in his famous speech to at least leave a curse rather than a blessing on the people who had come to own the land and destroy his people. Leschi learned a different set of rules and thought he could beat the white man with defiance. He was killed.

Yet, even with the Indians either dead or locked into reservations, the owners of the land were not safe. The Chinese had to be dealt with. Next, the dumb Swede and Norwegian loggers, who came out of the lumber camps and into town. And then all sorts of Communists, followed by the Japanese, then the blacks, then the Chicanos. An unending chore for the man who wants to keep his city clean.

Sometimes it's the major things that hurt, like the defiling of sacred Indian burial grounds, and sometimes the minor things, like gathering up small, precious possessions, which represent your life in your home. But, major or minor, it all amounts to the same thing: being robbed. It isn't easy to live on property that doesn't belong to you, property which, the first time you show a notion that it might be yours, you are told to leave.

Perhaps you can move into the University District in Seattle, which is now integrated, to the best of its abilities. When you walk around the campus, or on University Way, or go into the coffee shops or taverns, you see mixed couples everywhere—but you also see senior citizens looking with disdain at what has happened to their neighborhood. They don't say much; they just look and save the words for the time when no one is around who might retaliate. You can hear a lot behind closed doors in Seattle, and most of it has to do with the blacks.

The older Chinese have mainly ghettoized themselves in a Chinatown in and around the area known as Old Seattle. And, although the new domed stadium will tear down some of their houses, most will be content to look for other dwellings in the same area. The younger Chinese and Japanese seem to prefer the University District. There they are accepted, even if they are bartenders; when off duty, they are easily mistaken for students. They share apartments and lives with whites. They are assimilated into a peer group. Everybody goes to the same barber, the same clothing store, the same restaurant. And everybody maintains their cool.

And, if the great American statement "They're all like that" is delivered, sotto voce, at a bar, they know the man is speaking of waitresses or bartenders, not Orientals. A small dividend, but one that pays off in a feeling of freedom. They can go to school oppressed or work oppressed, but off the job or away from the classroom life can work for them.

The blacks are a different story. Seattle blacks don't mix in quite so easily.

To quote *Seattle* magazine from June, 1968:

> That small fraction of Seattle Negroes who have entered the middle class usually encounter a more subtle racism than impoverished blacks do. Take the case of Mrs. Mabel Atwood, as she will be called here. Mrs. Atwood works as executive secretary for a leading Seattle businessman. In all but her color, which is walnut, she looks and sounds white: she is groomed as quietly and

carefully as she speaks—Lena Horne to her fingertips. Yet, in both her private and business life, Mrs. Atwood encounters constant racial indignities.

As a child, Mrs. Atwood was sent to private Catholic schools here and in the East. "We were poor," she recalls, "so I can't explain what compelled my mother to set the standards she did. We ate dinner on linen tablecloths, and we used silver utensils from Good Will. She taught me self-respect. I grew up not as a Negro but as an American of African ancestry—part of the mainstream. That's how I feel today. In my business life, I encounter few Negroes, and in my private life, none. *I* am white, but my skin is black."

Uncomfortable in Seattle's Negro community, from which she feels largely cut off, Mrs. Atwood feels equally uncomfortable among whites because, as she explains, "They can't pigeonhole me, and they don't know how to *absorb* me." In her experience, two types of white racism are especially prevalent. One is to insult her with unwarranted compliments, such as these: many whites have remarked on her good diction, as though they expect well-educated Negroes to speak like cotton-pickers. Moreover, her nine-year old son, who attends public school in a white neighborhood, has behavior patterns no different than most of his classmates, yet his conduct is frequently singled out as exemplary, simply, says Mrs. Atwood, "because he is regarded as an exceptional *Negro* child."

At her office, white racism takes a different form— mostly, though not always, the deeds of omission. "In some cases," she says, "secretaries don't even respond when I say good-morning. I'm not invited if a group of girls goes out for a drink, nor am I included when there's a lunch for someone who's leaving the company—but I can assure you, I'm always solicited for the going-away present."

The upshot is that Mrs. Atwood holds her distance

from most of her white colleagues. She is especially wary
of one highly placed white executive who, as she deli-
cately puts it, "had to be told to refrain from putting his
hands on me, even though he had been able to restrain
himself with white-skinned women in our office."

That was in 1968. Warren Holtz tells a story about selling
a house to a mixed couple (black man, white woman) in a
previously all-white neighborhood around the Sand Point
area in Seattle. The man had a respectable job and there
were no financial problems surrounding the deal. It was
made and they moved in. The only problem was that the
former owners of the house had not met the new owners.
(The house had belonged to the mother of the wife of the
couple who sold it, and when she died, they decided to sell
quickly. Holtz found the buyers.)

The problem came when the new owners decided to
throw a moving-in party. The previous owners received
phone call after phone call about the thousands of giant
aborigines wandering about the neighborhood. The wife
collapsed, not once but twice, and was carted off to the
hospital screaming, "That black man is sleeping in the bed
my mother died in."

This was in the summer of 1972. Holtz tells more stories
about 1972 and 1973:

> I'll give you an example of what you might call
> black influence here in Seattle. When I was working
> at Best, we were selling a great number of FHA
> houses, houses to FHA buyers, and the FHA of
> course is an arm of the government and they are
> very, very slow at processing anything. On those
> occasions when we needed a mortgage application
> processed in a hurry, we would just call down to the
> FHA, introduce ourselves as Mr. Jones buying a

house through Best Realty. We would do this with a very thick black accent and nine times out of ten that application would be processed immediately.

Another story occurred in September of this year. It was on a Saturday morning, early, about nine o'clock, and there were four of us sitting in the office here and the chief of police . . . pulled up in front of the office in his car and in the back seat he had an enormous German police dog. He came in and he told us all, he said, "I want you to meet someone," so he went back out to the car, brought this beast in and introduced us to "George" and in all seriousness said, "By the way, he just loves to bite niggers and hippies." Could you imagine, the chief of police? He said he gives him a chance to feed on them whenever possible. I couldn't believe it, but that's our chief of police. By the way, he was re-elected this year.

There are blocks that can't be busted. But as the blacks get money they move relentlessly up the shore of Lake Washington, toward the Montlake Bridge, and beyond, around Northgate, Seattle's first super shopping center.

Seattle was hit hard by the influx of blacks brought about by World War II. The city needed them then and needed them even more as Boeing geared itself into a vast machine of progress, dragging the city in its wake. But the sons of broom-pushers and window-washers wanted more than their fathers were able to get, just as any American does. Some of these sons went to school and got degrees, and then the sons decided to drop out. They refused to be "tamed."

"Rip-off" and "pig" became part of Seattle's vocabulary. Not so unusual, except for the style Seattle's blacks chose to use. Pigs were pigs because they seemed to the young blacks to be hunting them, whether they actually were or not. The Black Panthers and Panther sympathizers who chose to remain in the Central District went to their favorite hangouts defensively, knowing that the police would be staking out the joints. And, if anything happened in any of the places, they knew full well that they would be blamed and beaten. But they still went there. They also went uptown, to the university campus, where the dropped-out Panthers formed an alliance with the Black Students' Union. It was an easy alliance. The BSU was ready, just as the labor movement was ready for the Wobblies in 1919, and Seattle was ready to be scared once again. The city had never really thought of blacks as a problem. And here they were noisy and a problem; black labor organizer Tyree Scott wouldn't cause as much trouble as Chief Leschi did; all Scott asked for were jobs on construction gangs. He didn't want to overthrow the unions, much less the government. But when blacks who had no education got together with blacks who were busy learning the white man's ways to success, things were bound to happen. As Larry Gossett of the BSU said to *Seattle* magazine in June, 1968:

> In general, the Black Students' Union is a political organization set up to serve the wants and needs of black students in white campuses. The educational system is geared for white, middle-class kids, so it's never served black students. We're educated to fit into some nonexistent slot in white society, rather than to be responsive to the needs of our brothers in the ghetto. To combat this, one thing we want to do is establish courses in Afro-American culture and history.

Coupled with the anger of the "brothers in the ghetto" and the actions of Tyree Scott, the BSU helped to make Seattle aware that there were disenchanted blacks in the heart of the city who could not be ignored or shipped elsewhere. The blacks had learned something that minority groups before them had never had the chance, or the education, to learn: the power of political action and a feeling for the climate of the times. Like those who brought to birth the Seattle Spirit, they knew which way the wind was blowing. They were learning the laws of the land.

If the Orientals were content to ghettoize or quietly be assimilated, and the angry poor whites to hide in bitterness, the blacks made the most of the ultimate weapon—movement. For some this meant housing, for some jobs, for all recognition: getting away from the broom handle as the culmination of existence.

In the summer of 1973, a friend invited me to a Fourth of July party given by friends of his in the Highlands, an extremely exclusive section of Seattle. I thought it would be great—swimming, food, fun. I had met the host of the party years before and, although we didn't know each other well, I thought we were at least on a first-name basis. When I arrived at the party, my friend who had told me to come caught me at the entrance to the pool and said, "Wait a minute! Come in here." He put me in a shower stall, fully clothed, and I stood there while he went out to clear me. He came back and told me that the host's mother had said, "We don't know him," and he then asked me to wait in my car and he'd come out and explain it all. He did—but he didn't need to. My car was parked outside the fence surrounding the property. As I sat there waiting for him, I found myself thinking, "My God! I'm a nigger!"

Granted the Highlands is posh—it stinks of rotten, expensive wood—so I wasn't as angry at their rejecting a shabbily dressed white man like me as I was at my own reaction to it all. The first thing I could think of was "nigger." What training can do to you.

But then I never knew "them." Nor did Seattle. I knew one black in high school and everybody was scared of him.

He had the same last name I did and, one time when my parents went on a trip, he stayed in my house. He slept in my parents' bed, and every morning when I woke him up, I thought, "What would they think, if they knew?" It was part self-mockery and part fear. I didn't know how to get him out of the house. Finally I had to tell him that I was going out of town—and I drove him home, in my father's Chrysler, to his shack.

I was scared all the way.

Now Seattle knows them, and so do I. Like it or not, they are here to stay. And they know how to stay.

It's not brute force, nor is it submission. It's what one could call gut-fighting on all fronts. It amounts to the recognition of the human in human being.

That is a difficult thing to accomplish in a city like Seattle. The city is composed of districts, not areas like New York's West Side/East Side, or Chicago's North Side/South Side. Initially, after the city had moved beyond the original plats of the Denny party, these districts were identified by the hills (Queen Anne, Magnolia, and so forth); now there are more subtle and defined identifications. The Central District (or area), composed mostly of Orientals and blacks, reaches from the Montlake Bridge, gateway to the University District, to the fringe of the downtown area and almost as far south as Seward Park. There is Windermere, Sand Point, Shoreline, Richmond Beach, Roosevelt, Mountlake Terrace, Lake Forest Park. And many, many more. Each with its own distinctive character.

And there is the Highlands. The Highlands holds a special fascination for me, and not just because I was fenced out. The Highlands exists behind a fence, perhaps because it is the last bastion of Seattle Family. Behind its fences, its residents have their own private schools (not parochial), their own churches, their own golf course. Chauffeurs drive the patriarchs to their offices and pick them up at their clubs, depositing them at their doorsteps and then departing gracefully until the next morning. Occasionally, I suppose, the residents have to leave the enclave to shop, but no more often than is pleasurable—food deliveries are much more convenient than facing the market. It is a part of Greater Seattle, yet no one may enter without invitation. Along with Broadmoor, the Highlands represents Seattle's gesture to the walled-in, self-destruct communities of America's future.

Not all the areas of Seattle are like the Highlands; they can't afford to be. Magnolia, for instance, has tried to hide behind CAMB (Citizens Against Mandatory Bussing) to stop bussing of students, but even that can't last forever. Eventually the city will be integrated. Money still talks in Seattle, and the Queen City of the Northwest has always been amenable to that type of conversation. There is a black surgeon living in a $75,000 home looking out on Lake Washington in the Sand Point area, and there are more like him to come. Affluence, costumes, and degrees are all it takes. The hardy hangers-on, if they can make a buck, always find a place to live. They may not be respected or liked by the establishment, but they cannot be kept out forever.

But the difference between a $75,000 house and a $75-a-month broken-down apartment is still vast, and while some blacks scratch their way up the ladder of success, many more of the brothers sit around watching the cops watch them. There may be a brief hiatus in head-busting now, but it cannot last indefinitely. Violence will flare up again and again until Seattle realizes that it is a city. Far from its rough-and-ready days, when the unwashed and unwanted were shipped out, Seattle has developed a tendency to put a lid on things. Some people pretend that problems don't exist; others work in a very quiet way either to promulgate or eradicate them.

Take, for instance, the Glendale Golf Club, established as *the* Jewish Country Club, which almost went out of business because Jews wanted to belong to an integrated club. So they set about recruiting goyim, and then black members. Only four or five blacks may belong at this writing, and probably not many more white Christians, but the club has proved its point. People can want to be with people.

It isn't so strange that this should come from Seattle's Jews. The business community, although monitored by the rich Gentiles, is largely run by Jews, people who had to fight through the barbed wire of the establishment to get toe holds in the land. It still isn't easy to be Jewish in Seattle; many doors remain closed and there is no real sense of the Jewish communal pride that one encounters in New York. Many Jews, not content to be businessmen and aspiring to the higher glory of the professions, try to "pass." To a large extent they still go undetected.

If you're invited to a party in Seattle the host will say, "I feel I should tell you that there will be a black [Jew, Oriental, Chicano] here." You can decline the invitation gracefully, or you can accept, prepared to condescend. There is very little "wildcatting" done, because among the affluent and the intelligentsia everyone knows the rules of the racial game. Only a boor would not forewarn.

Yet Seattle cannot foresee every problem it will have to face. Who would ever have dreamed that Chicanos would descend on the city? They were thought to be safely out of range picking grapes in California, or peas in Walla Walla, or potatoes and hops in the land east of the mountains, not wanting to live in Seattle. Yet, as Roberto Maestas said (in an interview with Stephen H. Dunphy in the Seattle *Times* of December 31, 1972), when his migration was almost completed and he found himself in the Yakima Valley, he felt "a strong desire to see the edge of the ocean. I couldn't conceive of it." Not so different from the feelings of Lewis and Clark.

There are not many Chicanos in Seattle. But those who are there have learned from the blacks and Indians. To quote Dunphy, talking about Maestas:

> He said he learned many good lessons in those days, lessons about community, organizing, cooperation and the oldest of all lessons: I'll scratch your back if you'll scratch mine.
>
> Chicanos have helped and supported the Indians at Frank's Landing. They marched and were arrested this past summer with the United Construction Workers Association [Tyree Scott's group]. So it was not surprising that when they had decided the only way to get action on their center was to occupy it, they had the support of most of Seattle's minority community.

Their center was the old Beacon Hill Elementary School, and on October 11, 1972, the Chicanos moved in. They picked a new name, El Centro de la Raza. The purpose of the center was to be similar to that of the Indian Center, with facilities for education, rehabilitation, and job-finding. Also, it would be a community center for cultural work and social activities. The sit-in and hunger strike were just part of the total action the Chicanos were willing to undertake. Maestas knew that pressure had to be put on the establishment, legal avenues had to be followed, the massive joke of federal grants pursued, bureaucracy dealt with.

All this takes time, something very few minority groups in Seattle have considered. Dealing with a massive power structure that doesn't want you to begin with can become horrifying, something that Roberto Maestas realized when he said in April, 1973, "We've been double-crossed." There are things like funding conditions to be met, and under those circumstances "please" doesn't mean a damn thing.

Seattle magazine, in April, 1968, described the Seattle establishment as being like the Cascade Mountains, "a series of separated peaks . . . *partially* visible some of the time and *completely* visible none of the time." From the vantage point of these peaks, Seattle's racial minorities are completely, physically visible at all times. Visible because they are not white. Yet even the Olympian disdain of racism can be ameliorated, if not overcome, because economic value is more important, in the eyes of a businessman, than skin color. Minorities must *sell* themselves, prove themselves to be permanently viable in the marketplace if they wish to remain in Seattle. It is an odious task—the rawest type of prostitution—but it can mean survival. And, to the unwanted, survival is the first if not the only step.

Porn

Arthur Denny wanted his city to be pure; Asa Mercer, the young and ambitious first president of the Territorial University, was so shocked at the co-habitation of loggers and Indian girls that he went all the way to the East Coast to bring back suitable mates. Unfortunately, neither man was able to control the lust of the men who followed them west. Pure in heart and pure in deed has never been a Seattle axiom.

Seattle was a pioneer logging and fishing town, and after the men finished one of Arthur Denny's fourteen- to sixteen-hour days, very few of them wanted to go straight home to bed. They felt a different kind of energy than that expended in Yesler's mill. For a time there was little they could do about it except find a willing Indian maid. Then things got better.

In 1861, a sharp San Francisco pimp named John Pennell arrived in Seattle. With a quick glance at the situation, he, like any true pioneer, sized things up and erected a house of ill repute on the tide-flats south of Yesler's mill. He called it the Illahee (Chinook for *earth*), but it was quickly dubbed the "Mad House." At first he was forced to use Indian girls, cleaning them up, making them stop washing their hair with urine, and throwing perfume and powder on them—for some reason the sweating loggers still felt that they smelled better than their darker companions; then, after the Civil War, Pennell was able to round up white rejects from the San Francisco brothels, and both he and Seattle were in business.

Pennell knew one thing that poor Asa Mercer never learned, that most of the lonely, horny loggers in Seattle didn't want to get married right away, that respectability was a word they'd never heard. And, although some patrons did marry their star of the evening, most were content to walk down from the mill for some simple dalliance.

But Pennell was just the start of formalized lust in Seattle; places like the Illahee flourished, yet Seattle became more sophisticated, more genteel in its desires.

So the advent of the box-houses, and of John Considine. Considine was "a teetotaler, a devout Roman Catholic, and a good family man." He was born in Chicago and educated in parochial schools. He briefly attended three colleges until the lure of a traveling stock company turned him into an actor. When he arrived in Seattle in 1889, he was twenty-one and broke. Young, out-of-work actors starved to death in American tank-towns of the 1880s, but Considine was different from the ordinary. He looked substantial (big-boned, just under six feet tall), talked impressively, and wore dark suits and white gloves. He had style and the illusion of class; he acted the part of a young man of means and ambition.

He went to work at the People's Theatre, a profitable box-house. Murray Morgan in *Skid Road* describes the People's and the box-house type of entertainment:

> Like other box-houses along the Skid Road, the People's made its profits not from admissions, which usually started at ten cents, but from the liquor sold to patrons as they watched the show, and from the card tables. The girls who took part in the variety acts were expected to spend their offstage time circulating among the customers, tolling them to the bar. For every drink they cozened a customer into taking, the girls received a metal tag, which the management redeemed in cash. If the girls wished to peddle more personal wares, the management did not object. Few of the houses had cribs attached, but the box seats were deep and the waiters discreet; for the bashful, there were rooming houses nearby. Under such a system, most of the box-houses employed entertainers whose talents were not of the type to appear to the best advantage on a stage.

Within two years, Considine was manager of the People's, but running a thinly disguised whorehouse did not sit well with either his theatrical pretensions or his urge to make the money to match his manners. He began to upgrade the talent at the People's, making it classier than its competition. For a time his plan worked (at one point the People's was clearing over two thousand dollars a week), but, in 1894, the Seattle city council passed an ordinance banning the sale of liquor in theaters. This effectively, if temporarily, killed the box-house business; without money from the sale of drinks, the houses could not afford to pay for entertainment—the whole wild world of booze, music, and women seemed to split apart; box-houses could be theaters or whorehouse-saloons, but not both. Considine went to Spokane to try his experiment and then thought about raw, rugged Idaho, but he decided to check back on Seattle first.

When he came back in 1897, Seattle, newly opened by the Alaska gold rush, was ready for what his particular talents had to offer. Not that Considine was a genius, but he had that same talent for sensing a profit that so many Seattleites before and after him have possessed. He sneaked in and quickly leased the People's Theatre (undercutting the current tenants, who had only a verbal agreement with the absentee owners). With the ring of the Klondike gold resonating throughout Seattle, he could bring culture *and* action to the town, and in the process make himself a very rich man.

He took the awkward hookers off the stage, telling them to ply their trade at the bar and in the boxes. And he booked Little Egypt.

That did it.

Considine had a star, and top hats joined the hob-nailed boots in the audience. As the Seattle *Times* said, Little Egypt was "a charming woman, a pleasant conversationalist, and one who is well informed on current topics of the day." She was also one who had been arrested for dancing nude at a stage party in New York. Something for everyone.

But this mixture of class and skin was not the end. Considine wanted more respectability. He wanted out of the box-houses and away from any association with porn. He was, after all, an ice-water drinker and a good Catholic family man. Motion pictures got him off Skid Road and, in combination with vaudeville, made him rich.

In 1901 Seattle's first nickelodeon, La Petite, opened. In 1902, Edison's Unique, a movie theater with a stage large enough to hold an act, opened. John Considine bought a half-interest in the Unique and, leaving liquor and prostitutes behind him, moved his interests north of Yesler Way and into proper Seattle. He began a chain of movie and live-act (vaudeville) houses that would stretch from coast to coast. Also in 1902, a Greek immigrant named Alexander Pantages arrived in Seattle from Nome and opened a quick-turnover, low-overhead theater he called the Crystal. Thus began a rivalry that eventually saw Considine go broke (and later make another fortune producing movies in Los Angeles) and Pantages, in 1929, sell his theater chain for $24,000,000.

It seems strange that two nationwide theater chains should begin in Seattle, and yet, given the situation at the time and the desires of Considine and Pantages, what happened came about quite naturally. Seattle was in the middle of its incredible turn-of-the-century growth boom; the gold rush, the location of the Great Northern terminus, and the rapidly developing shipbuilding industry brought literally hundreds of thousands of people into the city within a twenty-year period. With the influx of new residents there was little or no social stability. Rootless, traditionless strangers needed entertainment, and for new families whorehouses and bars were hardly the answer. Seattle needed class: family shows and lots of them. Yet entertainers (except for the superstars who could demand and get whatever they wanted) were very cautious about leaving the big potential job market of the East Coast and traveling three thousand miles for two weeks' work (at best). They wanted more security and the only way to offer that was to guarantee work at various stops across the country. This both Considine and Pantages recognized—to quote Murray Morgan:

> Considine had entered the national entertainment scene in 1906 when he allied himself with Sullivan [Tim Sullivan—a Tammany power from New York]; the same year Pantages had begun to expand by buying out a

six-theater circuit that had lost its principal showplace in the San Francisco fire. By 1911 the Sullivan-Considine Circuit had become the first transcontinental, popular-priced vaudeville chain in America and could offer performers seventy weeks' continuous work; Pantages, the same year, made agreements with three Middle Western chains that let him offer sixty straight weeks.

The difference between the two men that enabled Pantages to win the battle of the theaters was very basic and very vast. Considine was a showman with a business sense and enormous theatrical and social pretensions—he wanted to be a cultural leader, respectable and wealthy. Pantages was a hard-working hustler who only wanted to be rich.

Pantages knew nothing about art and didn't want to learn. He had learned his trade in gold-rush-crazy Nome, and to him the booking of acts was a trade—nothing more. He went for the biggest name, regardless of the act, and he usually, by fair means or foul, got it. He treated theater the way any other successful Seattleite treated his chosen profession—like a good businessman.

Considine and Pantages made entertainment respectable in Seattle. "Something to do" changed from a release for mill hands' tensions to Saturday afternoon family shows. But porn didn't stop with the reformation of the box-houses into vaudeville showcases. Not in the slightest.

I remember, as a kid in Seattle, when I would walk down 1st Avenue to go to what we called the Magic Store (a place where you could buy marked cards, fart cushions, and other wonders of the imagination), looking in windows of the places where sailors hung out—Palaces of Pleasure with pinball machines, "special" magazines, and the dark room behind the curtain, where it said "21 only." At ten years old, how I wanted to be twenty-one.

All of a sudden I was, or at least I passed for it, and I could go through those magic curtains, with a dollar's worth of quarters in my hand, and inhale the cheap vapors of piped-in cologne, and squint, along with my lonely companions, at flickering visions of some girl vibrating in her underwear.

It was almost enough, in those days and at that age, when nobody knew very much and anything that smelled like perfume and didn't wear jockey shorts was very, very close to Paradise. Looking back on it, I can see how Pennell made a killing by perfuming his Indian girls at the Illahee.

It is all illusion, like the little boys' Magic Store where I thought I could buy tricks.

The new pornography is class, big-screen color. There is no room for the old gent sneaking in on a bright sunny day carrying a raincoat. He simply couldn't afford *Deep Throat* or the girl *Behind the Green Door*. It's all spic and span and respectable for those who can afford it. With the Mitchell Brothers imports from San Francisco, and the philosophical and artistic justification offered by publications such as *Playboy* and what *Rolling Stone* calls the Pubic Hair Papers, the movie business in Seattle is better than Considine or Pantages could ever have imagined it.

But for some, just pure, voyeur porn is not enough to satisfy the lust burning up their innards. Like those loggers John Pennell encountered back in 1861, they want a little of the real thing.

Years ago, when the morals of the East Coast collapsed and fell into the ocean off Fire Island, Seattle was still dickering about booze. Nowadays, Seattle, like a tardy little brother, is starting to catch up—what the city lacks in finesse, it more than makes up for in energy. A tough band of mid-twentieth-century pioneers went East to law school, or business school, worked for a few years in Boston or New York, and came back with a new discovery, almost as revolutionary for Seattle as electricity: the shared apartment. The Easterners thought that they had perfected it. Groups of up-and-coming young advertising executives, insurance men, or lawyers, already bored with their jobs, but more bored with the train trips to Scarsdale or Huntington and the wives and children they found waiting at the station, started to get apartments together: one night, late at the office of course, for Charlie, one for Sam, one for everyone.

New York may be great for such a notion, but Seattle is better. When the idea hit, the young executives racked their minds for a way to put it into operation. All they needed was a map of Seattle—and the commuter islands came into existence: Puget Sound is dotted with lovely islands, reachable only by boat. And the stories started coming: "No, honey, I don't mind the commuting at all, and think how great it would be for the kids. And for you. Not crowded in. Nature. Nice neighbors. A garden. And I can work outdoors on weekends." Ah, yes, a whole gaggle of new Sweetbriar Brides, back once more into the wilds.

And that first Monday morning, house up, furnished, and admired, kids in new, safe schools, wife with the car and a wifely kiss at the dock, how the newly commuting executive must have grinned. Just play it cozy for a while.

One fortyish insurance man told me that he had balled every secretary in the office. He said, "Do you know what that means?"

I said, "No."

He said, "Forty-five! Forty-five! And every one of them great. Great!"

He was in an apartment deal with some of his co-workers, but since he had a bit of seniority, he had the place for two nights a week—late work nights, and then he'd take a late boat home.

Not all executives or secretaries are so lucky. Lots of

them glut the bars after working hours. Most of the men are rookies starting off on make-believe expense accounts, and most of the women are aging a bit too much to have the boss waste his precious free time with them anymore. These are the ones who end up in the horror shows, waking up in a room with ten naked strangers on the floor, swearing to lay off the booze, then asking, "Where do you work?" Much like we used to ask, when I was a kid, "Where do you go to school?" when dancing with a girl at a mixer.

The open town versus the closed town has always been one of Seattle's favorite battlegrounds. And the battle has not been as simple as it might seem to an outsider. If one remembers that the founding fathers of Seattle were very young men who wanted to be businessmen, or "Capitalists" as Arthur Denny called them, amassing fortunes and building a city, while those who worked for them were only interested, in the main, in making money so that they could spend it, the battle lines become very clear indeed. As the original settlers became wealthy, and rich or ambitious men followed them into the fledgling city, they moved north, away from Yesler's mill and the crowd it attracted: transient laborers and sailors. The Skid Road (which was really just a giant slide used to get the trees from the hills down to the mill—it has since been bastardized in almost every major American city to Skid Row, meaning a place for derelicts, those on the skids, down on their luck) became a demilitarized zone; south of it was a no-man's-land for those with high collars, suits, and vests, just as the noncarriage trade never traveled north of it.

When Pennell arrived, he naturally set his sights south of the mill, and others like him followed suit. It was a surprisingly safe place to be. There were plenty of fights and occasional murders, but the police generally treated it as hallowed ground, content with a gentle skim off the top, except for times that the "respectable" citizens raised hell with them to crack down. An uneasy sort of peace reigned, until the advent of the box-houses and John Considine's discovery that class entertainment would sell to the element sequestered on the hill. The Klondike strike was to a large measure responsible for the breakdown of the Skid Road dividing line. Thousands of people passed through Seattle on their way to make their fortunes, while smart Seattle merchants stayed home, selling useless supplies at outrageous prices in order to make their own fortunes. At the same time, those fortune-hunters weren't all dummies —they didn't want to cross muddy old Skid Road in order to find relaxation before the arduous trip north, and when they came back with their sacks of gold, they sure as hell didn't want to risk getting rolled or killed for a turn in the hay with a San Francisco floozy. Class hit Seattle, and booze and whores started marching up 1st Avenue.

Bringing in Little Egypt was hardly a palliative. Respectable Seattle women did not want their husbands learning about such things, no matter how artistic. Excuses didn't work. Seattle was far from the executive apartment notion. And watching a notorious prostitute riding in a fancy carriage in their neighborhood infuriated the ladies of class. Mercer's girls simply got mad. God and the Devil hit Seattle simultaneously, and open war broke out.

It was Demon Rum that the closed-town people went after. Without its evil influence, men would stay home as they were supposed to, not go out like a bunch of dressed-up tomcats. Stop the sale of liquor, and the whores would magically disappear. That was one side of the argument. The other was that if Seattle wanted to continue to prosper, the city had to cater to all tastes. There were—as everyone for the open-town concept had to say, "unfortunately"— those who were driven toward unnatural desires.

For the closed-town advocates, the crossing of Skid Road came at a most unpropitious time. The gold dust from the

Klondike got into everyone's eyes, even the establishment's. The newly realized Seattle Spirit (brought about, supposedly, by the great fire but really there since Arthur Denny had built his first cabin) held no answer. The businessmen knew that Seattle was fast getting a reputation as the wildest town on the Coast, but they also knew they were getting richer by the minute. Without any outside interference, the decision would have been a snap for them: the dollar always wins out over conscience. Most of the members of the establishment had long ago forgotten Arthur Denny's abhorrence of spirits, and more than a few of them didn't object at all to a little high-class dalliance. But, connivers though they may have been in the marketplace, they had a lot to learn about conniving in front of the fireplace at home.

This inability of those on the ladder of wealth to combine commercial and domestic duplicity gave the closed-towners a real opportunity to try to clean things up. Women started marching, and fiery-eyed Reverend Mark Matthews brought to Seattle the religious zeal that Arthur Denny had so yearned for. It went like a see-saw for a while, from closed-town mayors to open-town mayors. Then two things happened to change the balance of power.

First was the General Strike of 1919. In spite of the fact that the strikers fed the people, kept the lights on and the hospitals open, the establishment locked itself in fear and loathing inside its mansions. There was suddenly a real danger. The saloons had to be shut down, and the prostitutes ran for safer harbor.

The open town was hit with a sledgehammer of fear, backed up by money.

The second happening was Prohibition. In some ways, I think Washington was hit harder than any other state by Prohibition, particularly Seattle. Seattle's internecine squabbles were usually resolved, in one way or another, by a mayoral election every two years, but with the federal government against them, the open-towners were really out of business.

When Prohibition ended, both Seattle and the State of Washington were not at all the same as before. State liquor stores—a nice way of saying graft—were installed; the state was dry on Sunday; opening and closing hours were strictly observed; there were places whose sales were limited to beer and wine; and if you drank in a cocktail lounge, there was a strict rule that you had to be observable by someone passing in the street, just in case you thought you might be getting away with a little illicit pleasure.

Whorehouses were still around, but the open ones were not in Seattle. They were stuck out in places like Aberdeen or Walla Walla and were subject to periodic closings by capricious mayors. One Walla Walla mayor closed them all down, despite the fact that the girls had been going for their weekly checkups, and almost drove the migrant Mexican laborers insane.

Seattle got its prostitutes back, but they had become beer-drunk chippies in cheap saloons, or hundred-dollar-a-nighters for the visiting firemen in the posh midtown hotels. The city got proud of itself. It was cleaned up and safe. The sailors got their peep-shows, the local yokels their stumblebum companions, and the rich their own treasures. Seattle was big and beautiful and anything smelling slightly rotten was swept out of sight into a corner of the barn.

The magnificent World's Fair that Seattle held, even though New York wouldn't recognize it as such, started smart Seattle businessmen thinking again. With thousands of tourists coming to their beautiful city, why send them down to Portland for a drink on Sunday? Too late for the Fair—but not too late for the city: open the bars on Sunday for a few hours?

Oddly, it was those old-time advocates of open-town policy who screeched loudest about Sunday drinking. They found themselves, for a time at least, almost holding hands with the W.C.T.U. Opening a saloon from two to eight hardly made sense; why pay a bartender a day's wages to serve a few glasses of beer and an occasional muscatel? The hotel-keepers naturally felt differently about the deal; it only made sense that more people would go out for an early Sunday dinner if they could have a few cocktails first, and it would stop the bitching from hotel guests.

The ranks were split. But by this time, Seattle and the state had learned the art of compromise. Wherever there was money to be made, scruples went out the window. Extend the hours—open at noon and close at midnight—and make everybody happy. It seems to be working. Of course, they don't make as much money on Sunday as they do on Saturday, because a lot of people have to rest themselves for Monday noon, but there are enough unhardy souls who don't sail, fish, or ski, and the golfers do their level best to keep the afternoons busy.

Not everybody's happy. Because, despite its recent elegant suburbanization, there are still plenty of elements of the wild and woolly frontier tank-town in the city. But a sort of delicate balance has been achieved, a little something for everyone. As long as there's no crackdown on porn, and the peep-shows and the movies are allowed to go on, and the whores are discreetly allowed to ply their trade, and the young secretaries are allowed to learn theirs, and public drunkenness does not become a capital crime, things seem good for those who want their pleasures, and seem to be priced at levels to suit any pocketbook.

But let policemen start picking up stockbrokers squinting into the afternoon, sitting on the curb out in front of the Washington Athletic Club, or start taking flashlights behind the magic curtain of the peep-shows, or start parking their cars, with the lights out, in front of neighborhood saloons at two in the morning. Let anyone try to really "close" the town again and the dark and sinister underside of the Seattle Spirit will no longer be pacified.

Take care, Seattle. The logger still lives in your midst, and as my brother would say, "The Swede comes down from the woods on Saturday night."

David Denny
and the Seafair Queen

Call her Miss Seafair since that's her title, but a Seafair queen she is and a Seafair queen she'll be for a solid year.

"I feel like a queen," said Jackie Dean just after her naming as Seafair's No. 1 Girl during the Patti Page Seafair show in the Seattle Center Arena last night.

"You feel like a queen no matter what they call 'em, even without a crown," burbled Jackie. "Little girls all want to be a Cinderella or a princess or a queen."

Jackie was the First Hill Improvement Club's Princess in the Miss Seafair competition. . . .

Jackie's parents, Mr. and Mrs. Charles Dean, 13557 First Avenue N.E. were the first to buss her joyfully when she broke free of well-wishers on the Arena stage.

"I just want to be happy; that's my goal in life," Miss Seafair said. "I'm going to teach, but if you're happy, everything else will fall into place. To be happy is just to enjoy the people I love, and have them love me."

For her, that takes in a lot of territory. She has two more years to go at Seattle University. She is an Ingraham High graduate and a cheerleader at S.U. She says she's learning to cook, is making a hooked rug, and specializes in work for the handicapped because they include her own "little sister," Kathy, 18.

"Being picked is my birthday present," said Jackie. "I was 20 on Wednesday and this very night Mike Venable—that's my boy friend —is 22!"

—Robert Heilman, Seattle *Times*, July 28, 1973

It's the 1973 Seattle Seafair with Patti Page and Tony Bennett catching up with the 1950s; because that's when this particular mania started, when a man named Stanley

Sayres and a boat called *Slo-Mo* grabbed the Gold Cup for unlimited hydroplane racing out of the mud of the Detroit River and brought it back to Seattle.

Much of the glamour has worn off the big unlimited hydroplane races, partially because the Gold Cup is no longer Seattle's and Seattle's alone (the 1973 Gold Cup was run on the Columbia River in the Tri-City area of Washington, and the big 1973 race in Seattle was billed as the World Championship Seafair Regatta), but there is still a great deal of excitement generated by the presence of the thunderboats at Seafair.

The big boats *are* impressive: anything that weighs over two tons, is over 28 feet long, capable of over 180 miles an hour on a straightaway and an average of better than 120 miles an hour for a 6-mile course has to be. And on race day in Seattle, almost everyone with access to a boat, a dollar, or a TV set watches.

But the big race is no longer the point of Seafair, if, indeed, it ever was. Seattle is not Louisville and a hydroplane race is not the Kentucky Derby. The race exists as a punctuation mark—the end of "The Week."

The festival of Seafair is what Seattle needed, not one more opportunity for national recognition but a chance for the city to go safely, legally mad. That is what "The Week" offers. Seafair Week usually lasts ten days, from a Friday night parade through the afternoon of the Sunday of the next week, but it represents the results of some six months' planning and spare-time work. The major events (parades, races, shows) are certainly big and well-staged enough to be worthy of any major city. But it is the grass-roots work that is unique to Seafair. The neighborhoods of Seattle are actually involved in the production of the festival. It may well be that the organization and direction of each neighborhood's activity, provided by the residents, resembles a Boeing Company junior-executive-training-program type of "responsible community leadership," but that is not as important as the feeling that everybody is involved. Everybody, from tiny children to stoop-sitting senior citizens, seems to be making costumes or decorating floats or grilling salmon. And everybody seems to be having fun—a bit close to the manic edge, perhaps, but fun. The competitions, strifes, and hatreds of Seattle's real world are translated into the farcical, wild but harmless actions of adults playing children playing adults' games. The failure becomes a pratfall; the drunk a demon lover; the desperate secretary a princess—and the city throws flowers and kisses to them all.

The city is beautiful, safe, and filled with laughter. For ten days. During "The Week" everything, from neighborhood flower shows to national championships, happens at the same time. And everything seems to have the same importance—one feels driven to go to every event.

To appreciate the enormity of Seafair, it is helpful to review the 1973 schedule of events. We start with the Patti Page Show and the coronation of Miss Seafair at the Seattle Center, on Friday, July 27, followed by two coronation balls at the Olympic Hotel (one for grownups, another for those too young to drink legally); then it really begins:

Saturday, July 28
8:30 P.M.—Seafair Torchlight Parade, ending with the Festival of Floats at Seattle Center. (This is all gauze and lights and beautiful and endless.)

Also, this very night, there was Tony Bennett giving his heart to San Francisco, from the Opera House in the same Center as the floats.

Sunday, July 29

All day—Blackfeet Encampment at Seattle Center. Arts and Crafts. And, Seafair "Bonspiel" (curling) at the Highland Ice Arena.

10 A.M.—Begonia Show at the Loyal Heights Recreation Center and the Arts and Crafts Fair at Bellevue Square.

11 A.M.–5 P.M.—Hobie Cat Regatta (Hobie Cats are strange-looking catamaranlike sailboats) at Golden Gardens Park on Puget Sound.

11:30 A.M.–6 P.M.—40th Annual Rainier District Pow Wow with parachute-jumping at Seward Park.

Noon—Seafair Grand Prix 225. A Le Mans–style start of a marathon 225-mile race for unlimited outboards on the hydro course on Lake Washington.

Noon–6 P.M.—Alki Kla-how-ya Festival. A community event with a traditional Indian salmon bake at Alki Point (Seattle's first home).

4 P.M.—Seafair Grand Parade: 110 units including 30 floats through downtown Seattle.

7:30 P.M.—"Raiders of the Plains," featuring nationally known Blackfeet Indian singers and dancers at the Seattle Center Playhouse.

Monday, July 30

All day—Blackfeet Encampment.

10 A.M.–6 P.M.—Model Boat Races at Green Lake. (No joke. The little boats are capable of going eighty miles an hour and their owners take them every bit as seriously as any driver of an unlimited hydroplane takes his craft. They come from all over for this event, from as far away as Japan. Fourteen "drivers" came from Hawaii alone.)

9 A.M.–3 P.M.—52nd National Lawn Bowling Tournament at Woodland and Jefferson parks.

Tuesday, July 31
7:30 P.M.—Greenwood District Parade. Even Seafairers have to rest once in a while.

Wednesday, August 1
All day—Des Moines Waterland Festival.
9 A.M.—Lawn Bowling Tournament.
10 A.M.–6 P.M.—Model Boat Races.
11 A.M.—United States Navy Fleet Welcome at Pier 91.
Noon—Seafair's First International Kite-Flying Tournament. Open to all ages, and for all types of kites, prizes. Volunteer Park.
Noon–4 P.M.—Unlimited hydroplane time trials begin. Escorted tours of the pit area. Lake Washington.
7:30 P.M.—University District Parade and Street Fair.

Thursday, August 2
All day—Des Moines Waterland Festival.
9 A.M.—Lawn Bowling Tournament.
10 A.M.–4 P.M.—Guided hydro-pit tours.
10 A.M.—Model Boat Races.
Noon—Kite-Flying Tournament.
Noon–9 P.M.—Magnolia Community Art Show.
5 P.M.–8 P.M.—Night hydro-pit tours.
7 P.M.—Lake City Community Kiddies Parade.
7 P.M.—Ballard Community Nordic Days Festival and Parade.

A little sidelight on Thursday, August 2, 1973. Back in 1898, John Considine, of box-house and movie fame, John Cort, and others involved in the "theater" business, got together on a Seattle dock and decided to break a musicians' strike. Moreover, they organized a club, the Independent Order of Good Things, with the handsome motto, "Skin 'Em."

That began the Eagles Lodge, and with a slightly saner banner saying, "Not God, heaven, hereafter, but man, earth, now," people across the nation flocked to the Aerie. The night of August 2, 1973, the Eagles came home to roost. Mike Wyne, writing in the Seattle *Times* of Friday, August 3, described it:

> The Seattle Center dinner last night for more than 5,000 Eagles may go down in history right along with the legends of Paul Bunyan.
>
> It was a giant affair in the Coliseum—the only place in town big enough to handle the crowd which attended the dinner and the Bob Hope show that followed.
>
> And at that, tables had to be set up in the lobby concourses for diners. (They saw the Hope show from the permanent upstairs seats in the Coliseum.)
>
> Howard Marquis, director of food services for Continental Hosts since June 7, was the man responsible for Seattle's largest sit-down dinner in memory.
>
> Marquis was planning a "small" dinner in the Exhibition Hall for more than 2,000 persons, when the Eagles informed him they wanted to have 5,000 for dinner, instead.
>
> "I heard this about 4:30 Wednesday afternoon," Marquis said. "It was quite a surprise. It was also fortunate the Coliseum was available."
>
> The next 24 hours were frantic at times for Marquis as additional waitresses, bus boys, bartenders, tables, silverware, linens and food had to be procured.
>
> "We had to scramble," Marquis said. "The food was the hardest because we are having a bit of a food shortage."
>
> As union officials scanned their waitress lists and regular waitresses had their friends, available from other jobs, call in, Marquis had his staff unload a warehouse of supplies and invade the Coliseum.

Trucks were dispatched to pick up some foods and suppliers were telephoned repeatedly to fill up the menu. By dinner time yesterday, there were 125 to 135 waitresses and about 100 bus boys on duty.

The menu included 3,150 Cornish game hens, 1,800 breasts of chicken, 16 prime-rib roasts (averaging 22 pounds each), 875 pounds of salad, 850 pounds of vegetables, 288 gallons of fruit, 480 gallons of coffee, 625 apple pies, 420 dozen rolls and 120 pounds of butter.

Some "bit of a food shortage." Tell that story to Neighbors in Need, or the people holding food stamps. Let 'em eat cake—or apple pie.

Back to Seafair.

Friday, August 3, 1973
All day—Waterland Festival.
9 A.M.–3 P.M.—Lawn Bowling Tournament.
10 A.M.—Wallingford District Kiddies Parade.
10 A.M.–5 P.M.—Hydro-pit tours.
10 A.M.–9 P.M.—Magnolia Outdoor Art Show.
Noon–4 P.M.—Unlimited hydroplane time trials.
2 P.M.–8 P.M.—Fuschia Funfair at Seattle Center's Flag Pavilion.
4 P.M.–8 P.M.—Lake City Salmon Bake. Parade at 7:30.
5 P.M.–8 P.M.—Night hydro-pit tours.

Saturday, August 4
All day—Waterland Festival. Parade at 6 P.M.
9 A.M.—Lawn Bowling Tournament.
10 A.M.—Hydro-pit tours.
10 A.M.—Model Boat Races.
10 A.M.—Fuschia Funfair.
10 A.M.—Magnolia Outdoor Art Show.
Noon—Fraternal Order of Eagles Convention Parade.
Noon—Unlimited hydroplane time trials.

Noon–6 P.M.—Seafair's First "Old-Timers' " Picnic. Entertainment, games, and music. At Woodland Park.

4 P.M.—Seafair's Festival of Boats Parade. A water parade of colorfully decorated boats along Lake Union and Lake Washington to the Stan Sayres Hydro-Pits.

4 P.M.–8 P.M.—Lake City Salmon Bake.

Sunday, August 5

All day—Waterland Festival.

8 A.M.–6 P.M.—Kennel Club Show at the Seattle Center Arena and Display Hall.

10 A.M.—Fuschia Funfair.

Noon—$50,000 Unlimited Hydroplane Race on Lake Washington.

7 P.M.–10 P.M.—40th Annual Rainier District Pow Wow, with fireworks and band music at Seward Park.

It warps the imagination and almost destroys the body trying to take it all in. And the formal events listed above merely skim the surface of Seafair. There are constant parties, climaxed by what must surely be the largest floating cocktail party in the world. There is a large boom set up in Lake Washington for the Seafair Unlimited Hydroplane Race and people pay for moorage privileges there. Some tie up the night before the race and most are there at dawn of race day. By race time, no one is sober. One person, for instance, in 1973, rented two large barges and, charging $5 a head, signed up 600 people. For the $5, you got six bands, unlimited beer and hot dogs, and Lord knows what else. There is also boat-hopping, much like house-hopping in the summer in the Hamptons or on Fire Island. People careen back and forth across the boom, and chances are very great that you will return on a different boat from the one that brought you. Fun and games.

There are the Seafair Clowns and Pirates, who eat and

drink free everywhere they go during "The Week." Middle-class businessmen during the off-season, they go berserk during Seafair, so berserk in fact they are asked to represent the city at other festivals in other cities.

And above all the grubbiness, noise, and hysteria reigns Miss Seafair, plastic and alone in her loveliness. Huddling wet and miserable, trying to escape the rain and cold of race day, or standing tall, proud, and gorgeous on her float, she is a queen, and all the others, be they drunken Pirates or visiting dignitaries, are her subjects. And no one knows it better than she.

That's what it's all about: being a Cinderella.

There have always been two sides of the coin in Seattle. If the Pirates go off to get drunk in Los Angeles, Miss Seafair parades across Washington in regal splendor, bestowing her favors on no one, her blessings on all. It is a Seattle tradition that Beauty and the Beast must dwell together.

But another face peers eerily out of the trees, another voice, barely whispering now, that things are not quite what they should be. To the Indian, that voice is Leschi's; to the white man, it has to be the faint murmur of David Denny.

Miss Seafair, at least 1973 vintage, is everything that American girlhood should aspire toward. She is the culmination of Mercer's dream when he brought his shipload of eastern girls West to meet and wed the sweaty loggers of Seattle. Reform them and keep them away from the Indians. A good idea. It has worked, at least partially—the loggers, or what have you, haven't stopped sweating—but the sweet scent of perfume wafts its way over the city and, like those first flowers planted by the Sweetbriar Bride, covers up the stench.

Almost.

Seattle, somehow, is a safe port for all sorts of freaks:

money freaks, nature freaks, beauty freaks, druggies, drunks, rich and poor alike. And they all surface during Seafair Week. It seems, for those few moments, that everyone is happy, or mad in the desperation for happiness. Black kids march, Oriental kids march, white kids march, and the police show off motorcycle tricks instead of billy clubs. There is no Central District, no domed stadium, no bussing problem—no nothing. The only worry is how high you can kick in the parades, or how you can garner enough flowers to make your float the most beautiful. Momentary peace. The horrible strife of a major city is translated into the fairyland mock violence of a bunch of paid clowns, who vent rage without doing damage outside the law. Everybody loves the Pirates as they rough them up. "Give 'em a drink," says a woman as she is being mauled by four or five drunk freaks. It's all in good fun. Fun it is. Watching a city go crazy in toto has to be. It's a vacation. No one pays attention to national or city problems until it's over. But then the Devil picks up his due.

He doesn't touch Miss Seafair. For a year, at least, Jackie Dean is sacred property, someone for disappointed secretaries in failing insurance companies to look at and say, "That could have been me," or for their almost-out-of-work bosses to admire from afar before they board their boats or cross their bridges to reach the suburban homes they've sold their hearts and livers to achieve, and then grab on to a martini, some meatloaf, and sleep.

These are the guys Old Lucifer pulls the joke on. The week was great, hail-fellow-well-met, but then it's eight o'clock on Monday and the almost dead desk is there and you can't even face that.

There are alternatives of course: Rosseline's 410, reputed to be the best drinking restaurant in Seattle, or the WAC. These are both respectable because stockbrokers go there. As everyone knows, the market in Seattle closes when the

market in New York does; with the three-hour time difference, Seattle's brokers get a good and legitimate edge on
their eastern colleagues. There you go. With Seafair over
and an understanding wife to pick you up, so long as your
job is not on the line, you can be juiced and home by three.

If you're among the lucky.

Not many are. Some think so, but then that funny smile
comes over the bosses' faces when they ask where you were
between the hours of noon and three and you can't claim
witnessing a Crucifixion, and they say goodbye with two
weeks' notice, and you have to call the wife early. Of a
sudden, you're in the Central District—whether you call it
Bellevue, or Vashon, or Whidbey, or Point-no-Point.

It's no joke. The massive layoff at Boeing following the
attrition of commercial aviation and the SST crash was
really just an enormous public display of an illness that has
been gnawing away at the city's innards since its birth.

When I was graduated from college in 1958, most Washington graduates moved to Seattle or, if they had been
graduated from the University of Washington, they stayed
there. Those who went on to medical school, law school, or
other professional schools invariably returned. Since then,
more and more middle-level executives in law firms,
brokerages, insurance agencies, and realty firms quietly
load up their briefcases and clean their desks for the last
time.

Seattle is reputed to have one of the highest, if not the
highest, suicide rates in the country. If true, it is no wonder. After fifteen or twenty years with one job, knowing
full well that he is either too old or too specially trained for
any other, it must be an extraordinary decision for a middle-class man to make, going home to face not only his
family, but his overextensions: his boat, his two cars, his
lovely home, his skiing cabin, the golf club, the symphony,
the lovely dinners. Boeing has a strange theory, yet it is one

to which most out-of-work executives subscribe: that it is easier to train a new, young, fresh face for a job than to recycle an old familiar one. So the fired man waits for a job exactly like his old one to open up, and not just at Boeing, but at all the satellite industries and the nonsatellite businesses, from law firms to realty offices. Or he kills himself.

Of course, during Seafair Week all of this is forgotten. The unemployed man can try to forget for a week what it was that happened to him. He doesn't need to drape himself morosely over a bar, nursing a beer until it goes flat (when he had become so used to laughing over his fifth martini), or sitting in his dark house hoping that the light of day doesn't bother him. It is all so crowded that no one has either the time or the inclination to ask him what he's "doing now." In this way Seafair is a respite, a time-out from agony. And it is a welcome one; during "The Week" people can smile, even laugh, without having to check both sides and the back first. Seafair Week makes one feel, particularly one who has been gone for a while, that Seattle really is in love with itself, that her people are all beautiful, and her festival the celebration of a perfect year of harmony and peace lived out against a startling backdrop of water and snow-peaked mountains rising out of the ground mist as far as the eye can see.

When I wandered through the week-long celebration in 1973, I found myself forgetting what I was there for. Dazzled by the beauty of Jackie Dean and her court riding high on the elaborate float, I started rooting for model boats, hoping to beat hell that a good wind would come for the Hobie Cats, and falling in love with Patti Page for the first time in over twenty years. And, at the big race itself, when Pride of Pay-n-Pac nosed out Miss Budweiser on the only miserable, rainy day of the whole week, I found myself envying the guys out drunk and screaming on the boom. It is so easy to get lost in Seafair, you have to have some sort of anchor to cling to.

Mine was David Denny. Every time I began to feel he might be a creation of my own imagination, I tried to remember that he was every bit as real as Patti Page, Bill Munson (the hydro drivers' driver), or Jackie Dean. I also remembered this:

> Explanation *in Dedication 'of Plat of Oak Lake Cemetery,* as laid off by David T. Denny and wife, recorded April 28, 1891, on page 80, vol. 7 of Plats.
>
> *Explanation*
> The object of the undersigned in laying out this tract of land as a cemetery is to furnish a burial place for those who need the same, irrespective of nationality, color, or previous condition of servitude, where the rich and the poor will be on an equality, where the tax gatherer and the book agent will not ply their vocation, and where interest of ten per cent per annum is not reckoned up and added to the principal every thirty days.
>
> [Signed] David T. Denny

David Denny's first gift of land, also a cemetery, later a park, was eventually pushed into Elliott Bay, marking the biggest land removal in the infant history of Seattle. It is now known as the Denny Regrade, a name I'm sure that David Denny would not have appreciated. But Oak Lake, now called Washelli, still remains, and, though not nearly so elegant as its neighbor Evergreen across Aurora, the bodies lie in peace.

I tried to think of David Denny during Seafair and I remembered his reaction to the great fire, where the citizens, seized at first by panic, began to bless the Lord for purifying their city: David Denny went down and looked at it. At least according to his terse diary, all he did was see it.

Seeing was probably enough. Remember that he was Seattle's first romantic; that he bothered to learn Indian tongues; that, kid or not, he stayed at Alki Point, while others headed off for cattle or settlers, or whatever. He was conned. He had a fortune; he was busted. He walked away. This is all basically hearsay; the man himself said little. He had Louisa Boren, the Sweetbriar Bride, Seattle's first Miss Seafair, and he held on to her in the midst of a pioneer logging camp filled with all the false naïveté of the grubby and the greedy, the worst and the best elements in a place where no one knew which was which. Yet he held fast— from a young kid to the last of the surviving pioneers—to the only things he had left: his dignity, and his respect for the dignity of others.

Seattle would not have come to be without that sick nineteen-year-old kid living alone on Alki Point, mooning over his sweetheart, stumbling around, feverish, worrying about a roof, yet unable to put it up until his brother came and built his own house.

He learned the Indian tongues so that he would not have to use that infernal Chinook jargon or force the Indians into the further indignity of speaking broken English. He was a steadfast friend of the Princess Angeline, the stumpy, painfully ugly daughter of Chief Sealth, quite the opposite of many of the other early settlers, who treated her as a menial. According to Sophie Frye Bass, David Denny treated the Princess so much differently that one day she shocked him terribly. David Denny was a tall, erect man, and when he went into town he dressed himself up and moved with dignity, not for show, but because that was the way he thought a man should look in town. On this one day, while strolling, the Princess Angeline ran up to him, threw her arms around him, and cried out, "God Damn you, Dave Denny! Oh, God Damn you!" What she meant, of course, was God bless you, but the Princess's command of English was less than perfect, and since she and Denny always conversed in her tongue, he was bound to be more than a little surprised.

Clinton A. Snowden, in his *History of Washington: The Rise and Progress of an American State,* has the following to say:

> In 1884 . . . a settler who was American born, or who had become a naturalized citizen, might take a homestead wherever he could find an unoccupied or unreserved part of the public domain. . . .
>
> The courage, the patriotism and the moderation of the early pioneers, who heroically forced their way through two thousand miles of wilderness, inhabited only by savages and wild beasts, [they] founded a government of their own, and they completed the national title to the country by a claim that could no longer be disputed or resisted.

Everywhere one turns, it's courage, enterprise, or industry, or better yet, a combination of all three. Except for David Denny's diaries. They are not filled with hoopla; rather they are reserved, taciturn, showing on the surface much of what the man himself must have shown. He "looked" at the great fire destroying his brother's city much as I imagine he would "look" at a Seafair parade today, on the surface showing nothing but inside wondering what was happening and what had happened to the corner of the wilderness he had wandered into.

David Denny doesn't fit into a history book. He was too quiet and perhaps too honest a child of nature to fit into the notion of progress that molds our country's history. Maybe sitting alone on Alki Point did something to him that we will never know about.

Not that David Denny was a hermit. It is easy and tempting to think of his life in terms of two periods of time, the lonely vigil at Alki Point and the last ten years alone with his wife in the woods, but in the long years in between he was very much a part of Seattle. He made a great deal of money, which he used to back such things as the water system, the lighting system, and the street railway. Then, when the financial panic of 1893 hit, his city and some have said his brother foreclosed on him, taking his every cent.

Mrs. Roberta Frye Watt says in her book *Four Wagons West:*

> Then, broken and sick and old, he turned again to the forest. All that he had left was a place in the wilderness that he had given to his daughter, out where Washelli is now. When he left his old city home for the last time, he said as he paused at the door, and sadly looked about, "I'll never look upon Seattle again." Then, like a sorrowing father turning his back upon an ungrateful child, he went out of the city to his humble home in the woods. The forest had given him shelter when he first came, the forest sheltered him and hid his wounded heart in the end.

Pretty sentimental, particularly coming from Arthur Denny's granddaughter. Arthur Denny himself wrote in *Pioneer Days on Puget Sound:*

> The object of all who came to Oregon in early times was to avail themselves of the privilege of a donation claim, and my opinion to-day [1888] is that every man and woman fully earned and merited all they got, but we have a small class of *very small* people here now who have no good word for the old settler that so bravely met every danger and privation, and by hard toil acquired, and careful economy, saved the means to make them comfort-

able during the decline of life. These, however, are degenerate scrubs, too cowardly to face the same dangers that our pioneer men and women did, and too lazy to perform an honest day's work if it would procure them a homestead in paradise. They would want the day reduced to eight hours and board thrown in.

I wonder what he said about his brother five years later.

Arthur Denny knew what he was after, and he also could sniff out a pantywaist a half a mile away. David Denny also knew what he was after, and it seems to have been quite a bit different from his brother's goal. David Denny certainly did not turn his back on money, but he never took care of it. David Denny learned the Indians' tongues because he wanted to; Arthur Denny never bothered to because he could control the Indians with his bulk and his faithful Tonto, Pat Kanim, at his side. David Denny simply got to know them.

Seattle has never been a genteel or even a gentle city. Witness Asa Mercer's desperate experience in bringing nice eastern girls West to save the lonely loggers from the comforting embraces of Indian maidens, or the Considine era of the box-houses, or the mad thirst for pornography today. It started as a logging camp, was and is a major seaport, and with the Klondike gold rush boomed like no city in America before it or after. But amid the demands of those fourteen- and sixteen-hour days at Yesler's mill, while Old Henry took up whittling, watching the others work, the cold glint of reason took form. Arthur Denny was not kidding when he said, "We were all Capitalists."

They were, a solid hard core who knew precisely what they were there for. Not to go out and fish in handmade canoes—that, although it might have meant survival for a while, was suicidal to a capitalist. The purpose in fishing was what you did with the fish once you caught them. The

Indians caught enough to eat and, maybe, trade. The white man saw so many fish in the water that the shape of a salmon changed into a dollar sign and the purpose of fishing became to "get as many as you can" before they run out, and then ship them out of town. The same with lumber: cut the trees down, cut them into pilings, and get them onto the ships. And back came money.

Lots of it. Some men were smart, diversified (like Boeing is doing now), put their eggs in many baskets, always realizing that they were *their* eggs—they survived. Others were not so wise.

Chief among these was David Denny. His money, no matter how much of it he accumulated, was not the end of the journey. He offered it up, as he offered himself up, and those in the know took the cash but not the man. This was only the beginning of knowledge in what *Seattle* magazine (a magazine doomed to failure from the outset because it scorned the establishment, whose advertising dollars made the existence of the magazine possible) dubbed, in the late 1960s, Pugetopolis—a great growth extending, for all intents and purposes, from Portland, Oregon, to Vancouver, British Columbia: a giant-sized, tree-laden version of the trip one takes from Washington, D.C., to Boston.

That's the romance in the man and, I suppose, the romance in the city. Not everyone can keep everything in focus all the time. The business establishment manages to, it even manages to control the mania of Seafair, but the rest of Seattle seems content to let the fat cats run the city. As long as they have jobs, or the hope for jobs, it's all right. And all agonies dissipate themselves under the ethereal glow of Jackie Dean.

Still there remains that spirit Chief Sealth talked about, and David Denny personified—the feeling that, somehow or other, the ground that new, expensive shoes tread upon is sacred, that bare feet feel it better, that it is experienced on beaches or in forests rather than on fortieth-floor carpets. And many of those who cling to Seattle, middle-class, fired, and broke, do so not out of masochism but because they love it. They want the mountains, the lakes, the Sound. They want the peace that the last remnants of the land can offer even the penniless.

That is why David Denny, rendered useless by the city he gave birth to on Alki Point, after witnessing the coup d'état his brother and the other capitalists gave to his dream, walked north into the woods of Washelli, instead of going back to Illinois, or down to Portland. He had become part of the land, joining with it, as the Indians had, in a pact of brotherhood, and he finally understood what the stones felt. There are a number of Seattleites, even today in Pugetopolis, who feel the same way.

But they can't walk far enough north anymore.

Progress and the control necessary to achieve it are always building in Seattle. From its very inception, the city has attracted to it men whose eyes arc firmly riveted on the future, who don't really care what the city looks like at the moment but see it twenty to thirty years hence. They have been sturdy men with a firm enough grip on reality to make their dreams work. The list of their names is endless. To cite just a few, beginning of course with Arthur Denny: Henry Yesler, Dexter Horton, James Thompson, Thomas Burke, Henry Broderick, William Boeing, Dave Beck, William Allen, Horace MacCurdy, Joshua Green. Notice that David Denny's name does not appear on this brief list, nor would it be likely to appear on any similar one. He had different dreams—not of civic grandeur and personal glory, but of a livable place, with water, lights, and ways to get around. Simple ideas, so simple in fact that other men could not resist grabbing them and making them grandiose, leaving David Denny on the roadside all but alone again in the woods.

No such fate awaits Jackie Dean; she has her week of pure glory, and then follows a year of artificial smiles and sunlight. Then, with luck, she will marry well and return each year to the scene of her greatest triumph: where they made her a queen, "no matter what they call 'em."

Seattle is rounded about with dreams and now Jacalyn Rae Dean stands as the realization of them all. She also stands for the two great illusions that Seattle seems hidebound to impose upon itself: possibility and equality. One can only pray that she never has to face the horrible truth that confronted David Denny in 1893 and, once Seafair Week is over, confronts thousands of Seattleites every day. Give to her happiness beyond her year, and give to bountiful, sad Seattle happiness in all its years.

And, if it's too late for David Denny, remember that he once walked in the city of Seattle, and, if Chief Sealth was right about spirits remaining in the land they loved, he may do so still.

A Note on the Type

The text of this book was set, via computer-driven cathode ray tube, in Janson, a recutting made directly from type cast from matrices long thought to have been made by the Dutchman Anton Janson, who was a practicing type founder in Leipzig during the years 1668-87. However, it has been conclusively demonstrated that these types are actually the work of Nicholas Kis (1650-1702), a Hungarian, who most probably learned his trade from the master Dutch type founder Dirk Voskens. The type is an excellent example of the influential and sturdy Dutch types that prevailed in England up to the time William Caslon developed his own incomparable designs from them.

Composed, printed, and bound by The Haddon Craftsmen Inc., Scranton, Pennsylvania.